Computer Anxiety and the
Use of Microcomputers in Management

Research for Business Decisions, No. 92

Richard N. Farmer, Series Editor

Professor of International Business
Indiana University

Other Titles in This Series

Computer Anxiety and the
Use of Microcomputers in Management

by
Geoffry S. Howard

UMI RESEARCH PRESS
Ann Arbor, Michigan

Produced and distributed by
UMI Research Press
an imprint of
University Microfilms, Inc.
Ann Arbor, Michigan 48106

Library of Congress Cataloging in Publication Data

Howard, Geoffry S.
 Computer anxiety and the use of microcomputers in
management.

   (Research for business decisions ; no. 92)
   Revision of thesis (D.B.A.)—Kent State University,
1984.
   Bibliography: p.
   Includes index.
   1. Management—Data processing—Psychological
aspects. 2. Computer literacy. I. Title. II. Series.
HD30.2.H69   1986   658.4'0028'5   86-6904
ISBN 0-8357-1759-3 (alk. paper)

Contents

Figures

Tables

Preface

Work on the computer anxiety study reported here was conducted between February of 1983 and January of 1984. Prior to that time various informal studies on the nature of computer anxiety had been performed, most of which were reported in popular business sources such as *Business Week* and *The Wall Street Journal,* and in computer industry trade papers such as *Computerworld.* The view of computer anxiety that emerged in these reports was a confusing and incomplete one. Collectively, these studies had concluded that computer anxiety, also variously referred to as cyberphobia, compuphobia, and terminal shock, occurred to some measurable degree in about one-third of the office workers surveyed, and that a small minority of people suffer physical manifestations of their fear, such as sweaty palms, mild nausea, and elevated pulse rates. One study by Annalyse Raub, a doctoral candidate at the University of Pennsylvania, found surprisingly high levels of computer anxiety among undergraduate students taking a programming course. The crucial shortcoming of all these studies was that they failed to develop much understanding of the causes of computer anxiety—its psychological roots were speculatively but not objectively investigated.

A clear understanding of the origins of computer anxiety is prerequisite to answering two key questions about the phenomenon:

1. Is computer anxiety a transitory problem that will disappear as the general population becomes more and more computer literate?
2. Is it possible to treat successfully serious cases of computer anxiety?

While the study reported in this book falls short of providing a full understanding of the psychological mechanism of computer anxiety, it provides far more knowledge than has been available in the past, particularly with respect to computer anxiety in managers. Based on the results here, it is concluded that the computer anxiety problem is here to stay. The fear seems to have deep psychological roots and to be related to the phenomenon of technological alienation; thus, a certain percentage of the population will always be susceptible to computer anxiety. In fact, Sanford Weinberg of Saint Joseph's University argues persuasively that the incidence of computer anxiety can be expected to *increase* over time because computer use is permeating virtually all work roles in all types of organization, and workers who either consciously or circumstantially have avoided computers in the past can avoid them no more. The study results also give some cause for optimism about the treatability of computer anxiety.

A great many unanswered or partially answered questions about the nature of computer anxiety still remain, and research is continuing. Researchers at George Mason University, for example, reported results of their Washington, D.C. area computer anxiety study in late 1985 in the *Washington Post,* and their findings about the incidence of computer anxiety were roughly in line with previous studies. I believe that the most productive future computer anxiety research will need to involve clinical psychologists and information systems specialists, and should be conducted in tightly controlled laboratory settings. Such work would yield a more precise understanding of the phenomenon and its origins than would further exploratory, empirical field research. It is reasonable to speculate that at least some aspects of computer anxiety are intimately related to our fundamental cognitive processes, and that computer anxiety is complementary to, and synergistic with paradigms such as analytic/heuristic, left brain/right brain, Type A/Type B personalities, technological alienation, mathematics anxiety, spatial orientation, and human information processing. Controlled clinical research can begin effectively to sort out this confusing array of influences on computer anxiety.

1

Introduction

Computers don't have teeth. Yet some people dread their bytes.
Frank James, *Wall Street Journal*

Microcomputers have come of age. Since the invention of the microprocessor in 1969 by Dr. Ted Hoff of Intel Corporation, microcomputers have evolved from technological curiosities to their present advanced stage of development. They are now recognized as powerful computing tools for both businesses and individuals.

Among their many uses, microcomputers are beginning to find their way into the offices of managers at all levels in all types of organizations. Although various studies have shown that microcomputer use by managers can lead to significant productivity gains, their introduction has met with resistance in many organizations. The reasons for this resistance must be identified, and its causes corrected, if businesses are to realize the productivity gains that could result from full acceptance of microcomputer usage by managers.

Two generic sources of this resistance have been identified. One might be a simple lack of knowledge about and awareness of the capabilities of microcomputers. A second source of resistance might be some managers' innate fear of computers, evoked, in this context, by microcomputers. Preliminary research in this area has shown the second source of resistance, computer anxiety, to be a surprisingly powerful and widespread psychological phenomenon. If so, this gives rise to the questions of what types of people suffer from computer anxiety and what, if anything, can be done to assuage their fears.

Since fear is often associated with the unknown, it would seem reasonable that computer anxiety could be largely overcome by a training course that would include opportunities for managers to gain "hands-on" experience with a microcomputer. But there is no proof of this. It may be that this fear is so strong in some managers that it creates a barrier to learning and attitude change about computers, so that no amount of training and experience will succeed in reversing their unfavorable attitudes toward microcomputers and their usefulness as management tools. The purpose of this study is to explore these issues.

Specifically, the study will pursue answers to the following questions.

1. What are managers' attitudes toward the usefulness of micro-computers as management tools? Can any factors be discovered that are significantly correlated with attitudes?
2. To what degree do managers suffer from computer anxiety? Can factors be discovered that are significantly correlated with computer anxiety in managers?
3. Can managers' attitudes toward the usefulness of microcomputers as management tools be changed significantly by a training session on microcomputers? What kinds of individuals are most susceptible to attitude change?
4. Does high computer anxiety appear to present a barrier to managers' attitude change as a result of a training session?
5. Are managers' levels of computer anxiety after a training session significantly different than before the training session?

These questions are explored in depth in this study using survey research and controlled experiment methodologies.

Computers and Productivity

Communications experts blame America's productivity slump not so much on the assembly line worker but on almost complete inattention to the productivity problems of white collar workers (Rout, 1982). Lawrence Rout's *Wall Street Journal* article reports that Harvey Poppel, a senior vice president at Booz, Allen and Hamilton Inc., has found that most managers spend 18% to 30% of their time on the marginally productive tasks of seeking information, seeking people, and scheduling. All of these activities can be done faster with the assistance of microcomputers in the "office of the future," freeing managers' time for more productive tasks. If increased automation holds the key to improvements in white collar productivity, and if improvements in white collar productivity hold the key to improved overall national productivity and an enhancement of America's competitive position vis-à-vis the rest of the world, then it is crucial that managers wholeheartedly accept microcomputers as useful management tools.

Some organizations have come to realize the importance of micro-computers to managers and have taken steps to encourage their use. First National Bank of Boston has opened an in-house Personal Computer Center

(Shaffer, 1982). The bank buys microcomputers in quantity and resells them to employees, passing along the quantity discount. Employees are also free to experiment with the various personal computers at the center, try out software, and even borrow machines to take home. The same article reports that Travelers Insurance Co. has opened a similar center. The company has recognized the potential productivity gains associated with managers' use of microcomputers. Ronald Coakley, director of the center, states that it "is a way for the company to guide these new uses of the computers, instead of fighting them. We expect a productivity explosion." General Foods and other corporations are giving away microcomputers to any top level managers who want them, encouraging them to take the machines home and experiment freely, hoping that on-the-job management applications for the small computers will indirectly result (Bralove, 1983).

As the productivity implications of managers' expanded use of microcomputers have begun to be understood and appreciated more broadly, some computer manufacturers have moved to take advantage of this newly emerging market. Intel Corp. has, for example, introduced a microcomputer designed to enable managers without extensive technical backgrounds to retrieve locally and analyze data from their companies' central mainframe computer (*Wall Street Journal,* October 7, 1982, p. 38). The system uses simple English commands to help managers retrieve information from Intel's System 2000 Database Management System, and is especially targeted at managers in corporate planning departments, inventory centers, hospitals, and personnel, accounting, and engineering departments. The sizable product development cost incurred by Intel underscores that company's expectation that managers will embrace computers for their personal use, recognizing the productivity gains that could result.

Management uses of microcomputers might include office automation systems, freestanding microcomputers, networks of microcomputers, microcomputers as sophisticated terminals of mainframe computers, or combinations of these. Regardless of the specific context of usage it is clear that improved white collar productivity depends heavily on managers' adoption of the new information-handling equipment that has been made possible by the growing power and declining costs of microcomputers.

Managers' Resistance to Using Microcomputers

In spite of the potential of microcomputer-based management tools for productivity improvement, many people have been surprisingly resistant to their adoption and use. Raub (1981) surveyed attitudes of college students toward computers and found that fear or anxiety about computers led to negative attitudes toward their use. Weinberg (1983) found in a similar study that corporate managers suffer an amazingly high incidence of fear of computers. Thus, it is not unreasonable to speculate that computer anxiety at least partially accounts for the resistance of managers to use of microcomputer-based management tools.

Interviews with managers reported in the business literature suggest that this resistance has three roots: psychological, educational, and operational. Psychological roots of computer anxiety derive from managers' personality characteristics. Some people are, for example, inherently more prone to anxiety, regardless of its origin. Educational roots should really be called "lack-of-knowledge" roots, because managers who know very little about computers are more likely to have anxiety about them. This is simply a manifestation of the widely studied idea of fear of the unknown. Operational roots result from simple mechanical problems such as the inability of some managers to type.

Psychological Roots of Computer Anxiety

Looking at specific examples of managers' psychologically based resistance, Alexander Pollock, a vice president of Continental Illinois National Bank and Trust company of Chicago, says that "I think most managers, including me, are talkers. I would rather talk than write" (Rout, 1982). Pollock's bank is attempting to move toward paperless offices by introducing microprocessor technology into the executive suite, but the machine in his office is unplugged and turned around facing the wall. His comment suggests that managers are generally more interested in "big-picture" heuristic thinking than in details. Reacting to claims that computers in offices can reduce the travel time and expense connected with meetings through the use of teleconferencing and electronic mail, one East Coast executive stated "But I like meetings. It's more than just comparing notes about the budget. There are more subtle things—getting comfortable with the boss, shooting the breeze with colleagues." Managers seem generally to be the kinds of people who need social contacts, suggesting that this psychological class of person will be more resistant to computers and may fear their introduction into the office.

The danger of bruising managerial egos is another source of psychologically based resistance. Bralove (1983) reports that "executives feel that sitting at a computer ill-suits the executive image. Secretaries type; managers feel foolish and unprofessional if they do." Another ego problem arises from the fact that most technologically competent computer people are still rather young. Bralove notes that "Many managers find asking a computer analyst half their age for help a daunting prospect." A vice president of a Canadian chemical company says that "These executives are used to dealing with division managers or controllers.... They were afraid some whiz kid would snow them." Bralove goes on to report that

To avoid this problem, many managers wander into computer stores and pump salesmen for intelligible information. A typical conversation with a salesman begins with the line: "I'm interested in a computer for my children." "You hear a lot about the kids and then all of a sudden they're asking you about 'critical path analysis,'" Theresa Benson, a Computerland saleswoman says, "Computers make executives nervous."

Managers' egos are sometimes fragile, and computers are threatening to those egos. Ego sensitivity is a psychological characteristic, and one would expect that a manager's attitude toward microcomputers as management tools would be partly influenced by his or her ego sensitivity.

Loss of control is another psychologically based fear that is sometimes associated with the use of computers. Rout (1982) reports that some years ago AT&T gave a vice president at Bell Laboratories a desktop computer device with a built-in follow-up capability. His subordinates felt they were under enormous time pressure to meet deadlines, knowing that the boss would never forget. An executive working under this vice president remarked that "Even when the follow up was appropriate and the computer automatically dispatched a note to the person who was overdue, it was totally impersonal. People reacted badly to the machine's doing something that a human being used to do." Use of the follow-up capability was discontinued after an unsatisfactory trial period. Rout says that this experience at AT&T illustrates one of the most disturbing aspects of computerization in managers' offices—it imposes its own structure. Managers and professionals have their own way of filing, doling out assignments, and reading mail. The computer narrows that freedom. The executive director of the Office Technology Research Group, Pasadena, tells in the Rout article of a marketing manager who has learned that business performance is best when each transaction is tailored to the special needs of each client. But when a computer is introduced, the flexibility to make special deals is greatly reduced and that marketing manager "develops an image of technology as structure and constraint." This loss of control creates a psychologically uncomfortable feeling in many managers, causing them to resist using microcomputer-based management tools.

The increased accessibility of executives that results from wide use of computers in their offices and from increasing use of portable computer devices is another source of fear and resistance due to loss of freedom and control. John Cianflone, a division head in the U.S. Army's Development and Readiness Command, began getting messages from low level employees as soon as his electronic mail computer was installed (Rout). He says that this puts inordinate pressure on first-line supervisors because their bosses already know about all the problems in their area. Because of the potential of such electronic mail systems for short-circuiting formal lines of communication and command, many executives have resisted their use altogether. Portable computers are also meeting resistance because of their tendency to limit a manager's freedom and control, because executives with portable machines can be reached anytime, anywhere, thus making it impossible to escape the pressure of the workplace simply by going home. Also, managers cannot avoid responding to messages when they are transmitted to a computer's display screen. For example, Rout reports that Randy Ivancio, a systems analyst for the Army relates that

> In the past I could have said that I was out of the office when the telephone rang, or I didn't get the message. But now the message is sitting there for everyone to see, including the sender. I don't have the chance not to respond.

This loss of control, in whichever of the above contexts it may occur, causes a psychologically uncomfortable feeling in many managers, leading to their resistance to using computers in their day-to-day management tasks.

Educational Roots of Computer Anxiety

In addition to psychologically based fears, lack of knowledge about computers also causes fear. One of the fears about computers that people— even among managers—express most commonly is that they will be replaced by a machine. Terms like "artificial intelligence" and "expert systems" are beginning to appear frequently in the popular and business press, and it is not unlikely that many managers fear that the computer's threat of ten years ago to jobs involving routine mechanical and clerical tasks has evolved into the present threat to management positions.

This fear is not entirely without foundation. Shaffer (1982) reports that a program called Dendral is better than any analytical chemist at determining molecular structure from spectroscopic data. Internist I, a medical diagnosis system, is quickly gaining fame by diagnosing ailments with accuracy that rivals an experienced physician's. The Federal Aviation Administration is supporting work on an artificially intelligent air traffic control system, and LEXIS is a database system that is widely used for legal research. If computers have invaded medicine, law, and science, then management tasks may not be far behind. At least this is the reasoning of many managers who resist using a microcomputer for assistance in managerial tasks.

Fears of being replaced by a machine are largely attributable to lack of knowledge about the capabilities of computers, because the expert systems mentioned above simply mimic human experts and are not particularly adaptable to change. Managers who are truly knowledgeable about computers appreciate their limitations, and realize that they are not yet effective substitutes for human experience and judgment, particularly in such a richly complex task as management.

Some managers simply fear computers as inhuman, incomprehensible machines. Wysocki (1979) reports that a vice president of an Illinois bank said, "I was terrified of that thing," in reference to a computer terminal that was installed a few feet from her desk. Within a few months, though, she had gained considerable knowledge about the terminal's use, and most of the fear had diminished.

Lack of knowledge of computer jargon is another source of intimidation and fear. Bralove (1983) notes a report by Booz, Allen, and Hamilton Inc., that about 90% of the nation's ten million professional managers are computer illiterates. The language of computing is unfamiliar to most such managers. They resist beginning to use computers simply because they do not understand even the most elementary jargon when it is used by consultants, peers, and teachers.

Related to the intimidation by the computer jargon is a fear on the part of many managers that they are already so far behind in learning about computers that it is hopeless to try to catch up. Thus they feel licked before they start, arguing that they will always be behind, no matter how much they can learn about computers. These managers read articles and newspaper reports about the now wide use of microcomputers in the public schools, even down to grade school level, and about preschoolers who can write programs in BASIC (Sandberg-Diment, 1982), and are understandably awed. Senior executives are especially sensitive to their lack of computer knowledge. Peter Keen, a Cambridge, Massachusetts computer consultant, observes that "You've got a whole generation of middle-managers who are being squeezed underneath by people who expect to use the (microcomputer) technology to give them an edge" (Bralove, 1983). This compression from below will continue to become more severe because of the increasing proportion of college graduates, in all disciplines, who attain substantial computer literacy. The president of Quinnipiac College, Hamden, Connecticut, for example, has committed all of the college's 2,300 students, faculty, and staff to computer literacy (Healion, 1983). And Richard Cyert of Carnegie-Mellon University requires that all entering freshmen have microcomputers. A similar edict is in force at Stanford University. The superior and ever growing computer literacy of young people is so intimidating to many managers that they feign disinterest in the computer revolution rather than suffer embarrassment because of their lack of knowledge.

Another contributor to computer anxiety that arises from lack of knowledge is the fear of pushing a wrong button and damaging either the machine or the contents of its "memory banks." Bralove (1983) writes that

Still another unexpressed fear stems from the widespread notion that computer systems are temperamental gadgets. Managers are afraid that a missed keystroke will result in a nasty headquarters memo that reads in effect: "Who was the jerk who blew up the system?"

Fears of this sort always accompany one's first attempt to operate a new machine or, for example, a new vehicle, but with computers the fear of inflicting harm seems especially intense because of the inhumanness and incomprehensibility of the machine. As managers gain knowledge and experience with computers, these fears should diminish as they realize that most software packages have elaborate built-in traps and safeguards that make inadvertent destruction of important data extremely difficult.

Operational Roots of Computer Anxiety

A third root of computer anxiety in managers arises from managers' fear of being unable to overcome simple operational problems, such as the inability to type. Joseph Ramellini, director of advanced office systems at CBS Inc., claims that when managers refuse to use computers in the office, or when they pretend to be disinterested, that what they really are saying is, "I'm scared that I'm not going to be able to use this right, and I'll look like a jerk" (Rout, 1982). Away from the scrutiny of colleagues, managers are less afraid to experiment with the use of a microcomputer, because mistakes and errors can be private failures rather than public embarrassments. Bralove (1983) tells of a Westinghouse Electric Co. vice president who experimented at home with a new computer system before using it at work because, as another corporate official said, "He didn't want to look like a dope in front of his staff." The same article highlights the operational problems and fears about a computer system in a Canadian chemical company.

> [I]nstallation of a financial-planning system stalled when a number of executives couldn't or wouldn't type. "The greatest barrier to overcome was the newness of simply sitting down at a terminal," one vice president recalls. "Executives wondered if it was an efficient use of their time to be searching for a 'p' on a keyboard."

Managers avoid personal use of computers to avoid the embarrassment connected with their inability to operate the machine. For many microcomputers this is as simple a problem as finding the on/off switch the first couple of times. Some managers feel that they can postpone their confrontation with keyboards by waiting for the development of processors that understand voice commands, but expert technologists do not foresee these capabilities in the near future.

Managers in large numbers have resisted personally using microcomputer-based devices as management tools. The preceding summary of interviews and informal surveys reported in the press suggests strongly that much of this resistance is due to fears connected with computers. These fears seem to be broadly classifiable as psychological, educational, or operational in character. Taken as a whole, these fears about computers have come to be popularly labeled as "computer anxiety."

The Concept of Computer Anxiety

Studies by Weinberg (1980) and Weinberg, English, and Mond (1981) have described computer anxiety, or cyberphobia, as a high anxiety response to interaction or anticipation of interaction with electronic data processing systems. *Next* magazine reported in 1981 that the incidence of computer anxiety is as high as 20% to 30% of the American work force. While Weinberg has studied the work force in general, and Raub (1981) has surveyed college students for computer anxiety, there have been no studies that specifically focus on the incidence of computer anxiety among managers. This study will contribute to knowledge about this latter issue.

Psychologists have studied the phenomenon of anxiety intensively since the time of Freud, but this research has not yet produced a broadly accepted theory of anxiety (Spielberger, 1966). A concomitant finding of this research that *has* been widely observed and accepted, however, is that physiological reactions often accompany anxiety (Lagina, 1971).

Physical reactions to computer anxiety appear frequently. In fact, approximately 5 percent of the subjects studied by Weinberg have had severe symptoms including nausea, vertigo, stomach aches, hysteria, and cold sweats (Titus, 1983). Weinberg has even measured pulse rates and other direct indicators of anxiety using galvanic skin response equipment and found strong evidence of anxiety in managers and students as they operated computer terminals. It appears from these studies and from subjective reports that the phenomenon of computer anxiety *does* exist, that its incidence is widespread, and that its impact on organizations is significant. This impact is especially important to profit-seeking business organizations because their ability to achieve many of the productivity gains needed to remain competitive depends on how effectively they use the newly available microcomputer-based management tools.

Before one can effectively study computer anxiety, a method must be developed to measure it. Psychologists have identified two approaches to measuring anxiety: objective and subjective measurement (Caplan and Jones, 1975). Objective techniques measure anxiety independently of a person's feelings and perceptions, and include physiological measures such as sweating, blood pressure, and heart rate. Subjective measurement techniques for measuring anxiety rely on self-reports. Caplan and Jones argue persuasively that subjective measures are better yardsticks of actual anxiety because anxiety has psychological origins, and that psychological symptoms of anxiety are often present when the physical, objective symptoms are not. It is how frightened or anxious a person *thinks* he or she may be rather than how frightened he or she really is that is important. Fear is a highly personal and subjective phenomenon. The present study will, on this basis, rely on subjective reports of computer anxiety using a questionnaire technique.

There is precedent for the self-report method of measuring computer anxiety. Raub (1981) surveyed college students in the Philadelphia area, measuring computer anxiety with an "Attitudes Toward Computers" questionnaire. The questionnaire proved to be an effective measure of the phenomenon, as confirmed by a principal-components factor analysis of the results. Raub's questionnaire confirms the usefulness of the self-report method of measurement of computer anxiety. This questionnaire was adapted for use as the computer anxiety measurement instrument in the present study, as explained in chapter 3.

Other computer anxiety research has been done by psychologist David Ledecky of the consulting firm of International Resource Development, Inc., Norwalk, Connecticut. Ledecky's work shows that computer anxiety takes three distinct forms: the general fear of working with computers, fear of failure in using them, and the fear of being replaced by a machine (Healion, 1983). The general fear of working with computers roughly parallels the operational roots discussed earlier, fear of failure in use parallels psychological roots and fear of being replaced reflects lack of knowledge about the limitations of the capabilities of computers (educational roots). Various studies, then, some of moderate scientific rigor and some purely suggestive, all point toward the existence of the aforementioned three roots of computer anxiety. Some people suffer computer anxiety more than others, though, and this opens the question of what characteristics of a person are related to his or her proneness to computer anxiety.

Correlates of Computer Anxiety

In an effort to understand some of the causes of computer anxiety, both Weinberg (1983) and Raub (1981) have studied correlates, and the results of these studies have been similar. Weinberg surveyed college students and managers, searching for links between age, sex, prior computer training, math anxiety, and trait anxiety. Regression analysis was used, with computer anxiety as the dependent variable and the suspected correlates as the independent variables. The rationale for inclusion of most of these variables is obvious. Older people are less likely to have computer training, and will probably be more uncomfortable with the machines. It is reasonable that the knowledge gained from prior computer training will reduce computer anxiety. Math anxiety is a much studied phenomenon that somewhat resembles computer anxiety. Themes's (1982) study of math anxiety found women much more susceptible to the phenomenon because of generations of socialization that discouraged them from pursuing interests in science, mathematics, technology, and other "men's areas." Accordingly, sex surfaces as a possible correlate of computer anxiety. And math anxiety itself refers to the natural tendency of a person to be anxious, and varies greatly from individual to individual (Spielberger, 1966). Those with high trait anxiety can be expected to be more susceptible to specific types of anxiety such as computer anxiety.

Weinberg's study included 439 individuals. Their responses to seven-point Likert-type questions provided measures of the dependent variable and the five independent variables. Regression analysis found significant correlation between computer anxiety and sex, prior computer training, and math anxiety.

The 1981 Raub study was similarly structured, except that an expanded list of independent variables was used: age, sex, computer experience, math anxiety, trait anxiety, mother's education, father's education, and college major of the respondent. Because four of the eight independent variables were found to violate the linearity assumptions of multiple regression, however, only computer experience, trait anxiety, math anxiety, and sex were included in Raub's regression analysis. Separate analyses were run for the males and females in the sample, and experience level and trait anxiety were found to be significant correlates of computer anxiety for men, while experience level and math anxiety were significant for women.

These studies suggest that older people, people with math anxiety, and people with no knowledge of computers are most likely to suffer computer anxiety. Neither study addresses the question of whether there are certain identifiable psychological types of people who are likely to experience computer anxiety. Weinberg in an April 8, 1983 personal interview with the author, suggested that a systematic study of these psychological correlates would be extremely helpful. There is a theoretical basis for the expectation that locus of control might relate to computer anxiety, as explained in chapter 2.

Individuals can be classified as either internal or external locus of control types. Internal locus of control types perceive that events are controlled by and are contingent upon their own behavior. External types feel that events result from luck, fate, chance, and are under the control of powerful others, or are simply unpredictable because of the great complexity of forces surrounding them (Rotter, 1966). It is reasonable to speculate that internal locus of control types will have confidence in their ability to master and control computers just as they have mastered other challenges. One would expect internals to exhibit a lower level of computer anxiety and more favorable attitudes toward computers than external locus of control personalities.

Cognition refers to the high level reasoning process by which people think. Different people exhibit distinctly different styles of thinking, or cognition, and many psychologists have classified the extreme styles as either analytic or heuristic (Davis, 1975). These classifications were adopted from the original theory of types (Jung, 1923). As Lucas (1981) explains, "heuristic decision makers are characterized by their tendency to look at entire problems while analytics focus more on details." Success in working with computers requires attention to detail, so it is reasonable to expect that analytic thinkers would have a lower incidence of computer anxiety than heuristic, "big picture" thinkers.

Since these two psychological variables have not previously been studied in connection with computer anxiety, and since there is reason to suspect that they might be significant predictors of the phenomenon, one of the objectives of the present study is to determine whether they are significant correlates of computer anxiety in the restricted population of interest (managers). A concomitant goal is to study the relationship between these psychological variables and the attitudes of managers toward the usefulness of microcomputers as management tools. These possible relationships are shown in schematic form in figure 1.

Having thus identified factors that might correlate with computer anxiety, the next logical step is to ask whether a treatment can be found that either improves the attitudes of managers toward microcomputers, reduces computer anxiety, or both.

Treating Computer Anxiety

As discussed earlier, the resistance of many managers to the adoption of microprocessor-based management tools has unfortunate implications for white collar productivity and the continued ability of American industry to remain competitive on a world scale. Computer anxiety is connected with this resistance. If a way can be found to reduce computer anxiety through treatment, then the overall picture for acceptance of microcomputers and for white collar productivity will be much brighter.

Examining the list of possible correlates of computer anxiety: sex, age, math anxiety, trait anxiety, knowledge about computers, locus of control, and cognitive style, only one variable is found that could perhaps be changed using a relatively modest treatment over a short period of time. It is relatively easy to impart additional knowledge about computers. Age and sex are demographic characteristics that are beyond control. Trait anxiety, locus of control, and cognitive style are psychological constants in individuals that can only be changed by years of psychoanalytic therapy, and even then only marginally. Themes (1982) found that significant reductions of math anxiety could be achieved using rational-emotive therapy, cognitive behavior modification, or a technique called math skills intervention. But these treatments required significant effort over an extended period of time, and there is no certainty

Figure 1. Computer Anxiety and Other Possible Correlates of
Managers' Attitudes toward Microcomputers

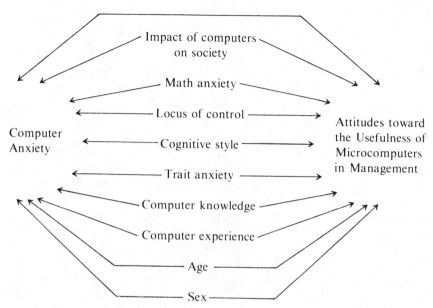

that reducing math anxiety will have a causal impact on reducing computer anxiety. Both Weinberg and Raub found computer knowledge to be a significant (inverse) correlate of computer anxiety, so it is reasonable to expect that a computer anxiety treatment designed to impart useful knowledge about computers might be successful.

This supposition is confirmed by Weinberg's experiences with treating computer anxiety, as reported by Paul (1982).

> It would seem that the proliferation of computers, particularly microcomputers, would lead to an increased level of computer literacy and, therefore, a reduction in cyberphobia. Weinberg said this is not the case. "Most people probably aren't getting educated about the problem," he said, adding that the computer education in high schools and colleges simply is inadequate.

The clear implication in this passage is that if knowledge *could* be effectively imparted, then computer anxiety (cyberphobia) could possibly be reduced. Weinberg advocates gradual, ever-increasing exposure as an effective treatment. In a corporate environment in the context of managers and microcomputers, this treatment translates to a training course on computers in general, microcomputers in particular, and hands-on experience so that managers can become personally acquainted with the power and ease of use of microcomputer-based software packages such as Lotus 1-2-3 and others.

Raub's 1981 research partially confirms the suspicion that computer knowledge will reduce computer anxiety. She measured computer anxiety in college students at the beginning of a semester and again at the end after a computer programming course, and found that the training significantly reduced operational fears concerning computers. Her recommendation was, though, that computer anxiety treatment begin not with a programming training course but rather with a general introductory course that emphasized hands-on usage of high level applications with obvious applicability to actual work situations.

The present study explores this issue of whether knowledge and experience can reduce anxiety and improve usage attitudes through a controlled experimental methodology. In the laboratory part of the study, a group of managers and executives were given a questionnaire to measure their attitudes about computers and fears regarding their use. Questions were asked that classify the individuals according to the psychological variables discussed earlier. Then the group was randomly and evenly split, with one group serving as a control and the second receiving a brief training course on the uses of microcomputers in business management. The questionnaires were then readministered and the changes in computer anxiety and attitudes toward computers analyzed. The results, as reported in chapter 4, have implications for the treatment of computer anxiety in managers.

Implications and Significance of the Study

The study contributes to understanding the computer anxiety phenomenon as it applies specifically to the user subpopulation of managers. Knowledge of the correlates of computer anxiety in this restricted subpopulation implies what kinds of treatment technique might be most effective. Additionally, the pre-post laboratory portion of the study indicates whether a brief training session can have any therapeutic effect on computer anxiety.

More specifically, the significance of the study is as follows.

1. The productivity gains that are critical to the competitiveness of American industry depend substantially on our ability to outmanage the competition. Microcomputers can increase management productivity. But this can only occur if managers' resistance to computers can be overcome. The study reveals the main correlates of management attitudes, giving guidance on what needs to be changed to change these attitudes.

2. The study confirms that computer anxiety is a significant inverse correlate of managers' attitudes toward microcomputers. Additionally, the study adds to the knowledge of computer anxiety by focusing on its correlates

in the population of managers, and by exploring, for the first time, the relationship between psychological types and computer anxiety.

3. The study discovered weak, but not statistically significant evidence that cognitive style correlates with computer anxiety. If a certain psychological type is in fact particularly prone to computer anxiety, then, given that it is not possible to change a person from one psychological type to another, this has important implications for personnel selection. If computer use and favorable computer attitudes become criteria for selection and advancement for managers, then early psychological testing might be able to identify managers who are likely to develop the desired positive computer attitudes.

4. The study found that a brief training course could not significantly improve managers' attitudes about microcomputers, nor could it reduce computer anxiety. This has implications for the way in which microcomputers should be promoted and marketed to business managers. Unless some way to change negative attitudes and assuage computer anxiety can be found, the size of the market for business-related microcomputers will be artificially limited to the subpopulation of managers who do *not* suffer from computer anxiety.

5. The study concluded that the amount of improvement in attitude toward microcomputers that results from a training course is no different for managers with high computer anxiety than for others. Thus it can be concluded that high computer anxiety does not appear to create a barrier to attitude change through training and knowledge. The implication of this finding for personnel selection would be that individuals with high computer anxiety may, through training, be able to adapt to a highly computerized environment.

6. The short training course that was not oriented toward programming did not successfully reduce computer anxiety, but the BASIC lecture in the control group increased it. This would suggest that early computer training courses offered both on campus and in the corporate setting should begin not with programming, but rather with a mild, nonthreatening exposure to packaged high level software.

The above issues are of interest to managers, corporate personnel administrators, aspiring executives, microcomputer marketers, and educators. Knowledge of managers' attitudes toward microcomputers and of the phenomenon of computer anxiety is significantly advanced by the study.

2

A Review of the Literature

Weinberg has described an incident in which a policeman developed such a complex about the computer console in his police car that he shot it.

Lois Paul, *Computerworld*

Various studies have established a potential link between the direct use of computers by managers in management tasks and white collar productivity, as was discussed in chapter 1. It was also shown, though, that the reluctance of many managers "to embrace computers often springs from one source: fear. Computers scare the daylights out of people unfamiliar with them. The technology is foreign. The language is often incomprehensible" (Bralove, 1983). This chapter focuses on literature relevant to the theoretical and practical aspects of this fear.

Anxiety Defined

There are various complementary definitions for anxiety, as summarized by Levitt (1967).

> A painful uneasiness of mind over an impending or anticipated ill....
>
> A danger signal felt and perceived by the conscious portion of the personality. It is produced by a threat from within the personality...with or without stimulation from...external situations....
>
> An unpleasant emotional state in which a present and continuing strong desire or drive seems likely to miss its goal; a fusion of fear with the anticipation of future evil....

Rollo May (1977) defines anxiety as "an apprehension cued off by a threat to some value that the individual holds essential to his existence as a personality." Caplan and Jones (1975) note that "the anxious person sees the danger as a threat either in the near future (e.g., at each proceeding second) or in the more distant future." The same authors relate that the anticipatory character of anxiety has been explained from various points of view (Brenner, 1953; Freud, 1926/1959; Lazarus and Averill, 1972), but that its future orientation is always mentioned as an important aspect of the phenomenon. Lazarus and Averill point out that anxiety accompanies states of ambiguity about the future. Lagina (1971) says that anxiety is "a state of heightened tension or a feeling of apprehensive expectation."

This collection of definitions and interpretations of anxiety suggests that there is no single, clear-cut, universally accepted definition of anxiety. As Levitt points out, "The range of possible definitions is, in principle, unlimited, and, in practice, very broad." Psychologists have debated the precise definition of anxiety for almost 80 years, and it is not likely that this debate will end soon. Ignoring semantic nuances and the fine points of psychological theory, however, there is a clear thread running through all these definitions, and that is that anxiety refers to fear about something in the future.

Fear about the future can be rational or irrational, and permanent or transitory, and these distinctions lead to the identification and definition of some subtypes of anxiety that are relatively widely accepted by psychologists. May says that when the apprehension is proportionate to the actual (objective) danger, the anxiety is "normal," but that if the apprehension is disproportionate to the objective danger, then the anxiety is "neurotic." Regarding the temporal aspects of anxiety, Spielberger (1966) distinguishes between trait anxiety and state anxiety—concepts that originated from factor analytic studies by Cattell and Scheier (1958). Trait anxiety refers to a person's basic tendency to be anxious. This is a personality characteristic (trait) that does not change significantly over time. State anxiety is a transitory condition that varies in intensity, fluctuates over time, and arises in response to a specific situation. Thus, we have a rough sort of four-way classification system for anxiety: it can be normal or neurotic in intensity and permanent or temporary in duration.

Of these four classifications, the present study is concerned mainly with the transitory-neurotic type of anxiety as it applies specifically to computers. In this context, then, we would define computer anxiety as "the tendency of a particular person to experience a level of uneasiness over his or her impending use of a computer, that is disproportionate to the actual threat presented by the computer." Of the four classes of computer anxiety, this is the most important because it is excessive in degree and arises whenever interaction with computers occurs. A manager who suffers from this type of computer anxiety is likely to experience difficulty in the workplace whenever computers are concerned. The other three classes of computer anxiety are considerably less debilitating and can even be expected to occur in people who are computing professionals.

Fox, Brody, and Tobin, 1980). Fox, Brody, and Tobin found that males with high math anxiety are likely to study mathematics in spite of their fear because of their perception of the importance of mathematics classes. It has also been found that parents, teachers, counselors, and peers unwittingly create sex role stereotypes that contribute to math anxiety and thus mathematics avoidance among girls (Fennema et al., 1981). Numerous researchers including Brush (1981) have found that pure dislike of mathematics is a cause of mathematics avoidance, and that mathematics dislike in girls grows faster with age than it does in boys.

Yet other explanations have been found. Junghans (1980) found that girls are inferior at problem solving because they have been socialized to be more conforming and more sensitive to the opinions of others, leading to a lack of confidence and to avoidance of the risk taking inherent in problem solving. Finally, it has been shown (Pedro et al., 1981) that girls tend to avoid situations in which they are likely to fail.

Clearly, a number of plausible explanations have been developed to try to explain math anxiety. Whatever its causes, however, the phenomenon is real. Significant sex differences have even been found on mathematics SAT scores (Benbow and Stanley, 1980). Some of this research in math anxiety has provided a starting point for the study of computer anxiety. In this vein, the correlates of math anxiety are worth examining to the extent that they might provide clues about the correlates of computer anxiety.

Correlates of Math Anxiety

Themes's review of the math anxiety literature (1982) identifies a number of correlates of math anxiety that various researchers discovered. Test anxiety has been found to correlate strongly with math anxiety; it has, in fact, been shown that math anxiety seems to be induced more by testing than by mathematics itself. Trait anxiety is another correlate. The reasoning here is that a person with high trait anxiety will be more susceptible to all kinds of anxiety: math anxiety, computer anxiety, snake anxiety. Other correlates of math anxiety, in addition to the primary correlate of sex, are years of high school mathematics, teachers' attitude toward mathematics, mathematics achievement, and age.

Although none of these factors can be proven to be causal, they all have been found to be correlated with math anxiety. Treating these factors might reduce math anxiety. To the extent that some of these factors can be shown to be correlates of the similar phenomenon of computer anxiety, treatments for computer anxiety are suggested.

Measurement

Measurement methods for math anxiety may contribute to the design of computer anxiety measurement instruments. Suinn (1972) developed an instrument called the Math Anxiety Rating Scale (MARS) that consists of 98 five-point Likert questions. Test-retest reliability of the instrument is .78 (Suinn). Construct validity has been shown through pre-post studies and factor analysis. Interestingly, one factor analysis (Resnick, Viehe, and Segal, 1982) yielded factors of evaluation anxiety, computation anxiety, and social responsibility anxiety. These factors roughly parallel, respectively, the proposed computer anxiety factors of psychological, operational, and knowledge discussed in chapter 5.

Another measure of math anxiety is the Mathematics Attitude Scale (MAS) (Fennema and Sherman, 1976). This scale consists of only ten five-point Likert questions. A reliability of .92 has been calculated for this instrument, using the split-half method (Betz, 1978).

The Syracuse Mathematics Anxiety Scale (Sudweeks et al., 1980) is an 18-item Likert-type questionnaire. Test-retest reliability using Cronbach's alpha is .95. A final instrument is called the Mathematics Confidence Scale (Dowling, 1978). Respondents are given 18 mathematics problems and asked to rate their confidence in solving each problem. The reliability and validity of this instrument have not yet been well established.

Raub's (1981) study of the correlates of computer anxiety included math anxiety as a correlate and used Fennema and Sherman's MAS. Raub also used this scale as a guide in developing the instrument to measure computer anxiety.

Treatment of Math Anxiety

Themes (1982) studied the three most popular methods of treating math anxiety. Two of the methods attempt modification of cognitive behavior, and the third uses a mathematics skills program to reduce math anxiety.

The first method, Albert Ellis's rational-emotive therapy (Ellis and Abrahams, 1978), uses the technique of disputing one's own irrational beliefs about mathematics. This method is designed for therapeutic efficiency and uses challenges such as, "What is the worst thing that could happen to me if this happens?" Meichenbaum's cognitive behavior modification (1977) is the second method. The technique suggests that one recognize negative self-statements, tell oneself more realistic, positive statements, and use relaxation techniques. This therapy is usually given in a small group. Mathematics skills intervention simply seeks to reduce fear by imparting knowledge. Bander, Russell, and Zamostny (1982) found that skills intervention yielded the greatest reduction in self-reported anxiety skills over the short run compared to cognitive treatments. Themes (1982) performed a quasi-experimental comparison of these three treatments with the result that all three significantly reduced math anxiety but with no significant difference among the success levels of the three treatments.

The success of the mathematics skills intervention justifies the proposition in the present study that a brief computer training session could potentially improve managers' attitudes toward microcomputers and reduce computer anxiety.

The research in math anxiety reported in this section provides a starting point for similar studies of computer anxiety. Also, there is evidence from this research that math anxiety may itself be a correlate of computer anxiety.

Research in Computer Anxiety

Research in computer anxiety is extremely sparse. Formal studies and reports are almost nonexistent. Aside from a handful of semiacademic studies, most of what is known about this topic must be gleaned from the popular business press and from personal experience and interviews.

Most of the formal work that has been done in the area has been performed by Dr. Sanford B. Weinberg when he was with Saint Joseph's University in Philadelphia. In addition to this formal work, Weinberg's name appears in virtually every article on the topic of computer anxiety, including pieces in the *Wall Street Journal, Computerworld, Interface Age,* and other publications. He has been interviewed on the topic on the CBS Evening News (CBS Inc., 1982). Weinberg also consults with industry on computer anxiety and other aspects of the human/computer interface.

In a meeting with the author in Philadelphia on April 8, 1983, Weinberg related that the genesis of the computer anxiety field occurred in 1978–79 when he was on the staff of the University of Connecticut. In the process of conducting research on various methods for teaching computer programming, it became apparent that significant numbers of people actually seemed to be afraid of computers beyond the usual low level anxiety that accompanies any new experience. His interest in this phenomenon grew, and he began to study the nature and incidence of computer anxiety, or, as he prefers to call it, cyberphobia.

The phenomenon is so new that there is not even an agreed-upon name. For example, David V. Cossey, director of the Wharton Computer Center at the University of Pennsylvania, has observed a condition in MBA students that he calls "terminal shock" (Titus, 1983). He speculates that the condition arises when students under pressure to learn to use computers suffer the frustration of being unable to control the machine. Healion (1983), reporting on the same phenomenon, uses the term "compuphobia." And Sandberg-Diment, writing in the *New York Times* in 1982, labels the condition "Computer Fear Syndrome." Regardless of the term used, however, it is clear that the same phenomenon is being described. For consistency, this study uses the term computer anxiety.

Although Weinberg is the recognized international expert on computer anxiety, relatively little of his work has been published because of long journal publication lags. Most of his work has been reported informally in business newspapers. James (1982) reports Weinberg's estimate that approximately 30% of the nation's office workers have some degree of computer anxiety. The incidence of the condition among managers is not, however, well known. Using interview techniques and even galvanic skin response equipment to study 523 college students and corporate managers over a four-year period, Weinberg found that nearly one-third of them suffered from computer anxiety. Severe symptoms show up in 5% of cases, including nausea, vertigo, and cold sweats.

In a 1982 article by Paul, Weinberg is reported to have remarked that many of the people found to have computer anxiety are those who opted for nontechnical jobs or careers such as clerical work, advertising, or sales, and now find themselves thrust unwillingly into a computerized environment. Weinberg says that "One of the major causes of the phobia is the feeling that you have lost control" (Paul, 1982). This statement justifies the inclusion of the locus of control psychological variable as a possible correlate, as will be discussed shortly.

One might speculate that computer anxiety is a transitory problem that will disappear as the current generation of school age youth, who are gaining computer exposure at an early age, move into the work force. Sandberg-Diment (1982) implies this view when he states that "For children, somehow, there is nothing intimidating whatsoever about a computer or programming it." But there is no evidence that this is true of *all* children.

Weinberg does not believe that computer anxiety is a transitory phenomenon, partly because the computer training and exposure that young people are getting in most high schools and colleges is inadequate. This is reflected in the fact that young and old alike are suffering from the problem. In fact, Weinberg feels that the current proliferation of microcomputers will, rather than reducing the incidence of computer anxiety by increasing computer literacy, lead to an even higher rate of computer anxiety as society becomes more and more computerized. Increasing numbers of people in totally nontechnical fields are now finding themselves confronted by computers. He notes that there will always, in any age, be a certain proportion of people with an aversion to technical topics and an inability to think in the disciplined, systematic way required for successful interaction with computers. Even people with prior computer experience sometimes suffer from the condition because of, for example, bad experiences with premature releases of faulty software packages, as Weinberg explains.

Other research in computer anxiety includes work on its correlates by Weinberg and English (1983), on treatment by Weinberg, English, and Mond (1981) and by Shapiro (1979), and on correlates in college students by Raub (1981). Raub's research is particularly valuable because it explores some of the fundamental origins of computer anxiety.

Origins of Computer Anxiety

Raub reports semiformal studies of computer attitudes by Ahl (1976) and Lichtman (1979) that sampled the general public and educators, respectively. Cluster analysis of the responses to Ahl's 17-item Likert questionnaire revealed four groups of responses ($N = 843$): computer impact on quality of life, computer threat to society, the role of computers, and the computer itself. Lichtman used a slightly modified version of the same questionnaire to survey educators. Although no statistical analysis was done, visual inspection of the plotted data suggests that the teacher sample reacts more negatively to computers than does the general public. This may be because many teachers view computer-aided instruction as a threat to their profession.

In a much more rigorous study, Lee (1970) performed a nationwide study of public views toward computers using a sample of 3,000 people aged 18 or older. Factor analysis of his ten-item questionnaire yielded two independent factors. As reported by Raub,

> Factor I, the Beneficial Tool of Man Perspective, described a positively-toned set of beliefs that computers are beneficial in science, industry, and business. This factor represented the majority view. Factor II, the Awesome Thinking Machine Perspective, captured the science-fiction view of the computer as an autonomous entity capable of superiority of human thought.

Lee's discussion focused on the second factor because of its potentially serious negative impact on society and on the computer industry.

Lee also gathered information on psychosocial attitudes. Alienation and intolerance of ambiguity accounted for 23% of the variance in Factor II, and education was found to be the strongest social class indicator of this factor. Since education seems to increase a person's ability to tolerate ambiguity and uncertainty, it would be fair to speculate that business managers and executives, given their relatively high level of education, would have somewhat less negative attitudes toward computers than the society as a whole. Lee's Awesome Thinking Machine Perspective connotes fear—fear of an incomprehensibly complex machine with capabilities far exceeding those of a human. This factor, which reflects ignorance about the capabilities and limitations of computers, is one of the generic origins of computer anxiety. Some managers may simply fear the awesome power of the machine, although one would think that this factor would be less pronounced with respect to a 30-pound desktop microcomputer than a room full of whirring mainframe computer equipment.

Raub's (1981) study of attitudes toward computers among college students included a factor analysis that revealed three items: appreciation of computers and a desire to learn more about them, computer usage anxiety, and fears about the computer's negative impact on society. The latter two reveal additional origins of computer anxiety. As discussed in chapter 1, some people seem to have a fear of simple operational failure, such as inability to type or fear of damaging the machine or its contents by pushing a wrong button. Others are afraid that computers will ultimately have a negative impact on society because, for example, they isolate people from one another and they threaten personal privacy.

Technological Alienation

Alienation from technology is a sense of being disconnected from the technological mainstream. Raub found that college students with high computer anxiety shared a background of little or no encouragement or necessity to learn about anything even remotely technical. Now that the requirement for computer literacy has been thrust upon such people, they feel "almost paralyzed by the challenge." It is easy to imagine that managers in certain nontechnical functional specialties such as sales and transportation might experience similar anxieties when confronted with computers.

A rigorous study of the impact of technological alienation on computer anxiety would, however, be of questionable theoretical validity. Robinson and Shaver (1973) have advised caution in using alienation scales because there is little empirical validation for the concept of alienation.

Fear of the Unknown

Another possible origin of computer anxiety that eludes precise psychometric measurement is fear of the unknown. Raub found in clinical interviews with high anxiety college students that such people are hesitant to participate in *any* activity where they had little knowledge of the possible outcome, including such commonplace activities as meeting new people. This fear of the untried and unknown is associated with fear of failure. Themes (1982) identified fear of failure as a correlate of math anxiety that was especially strong in women. One would not expect a particularly strong fear of failure in women managers, though, or these women would not have opted to enter the management work force in the first place.

Summarizing, the phenomenon of computer anxiety has been found tentatively to originate from fear of computers as awesome, superhuman thinking machines, from their possible negative impact on society, from fear of failure in their use, from general technological alienation, and from fear of the unknown.

These hypothesized factors have provided a basis for what little research has been performed to date into the possible correlates of computer anxiety.

Research into Correlates of Computer Anxiety

The research by Raub (1981) and Weinberg and English (1983), investigated math anxiety, sex, age, trait anxiety, and knowledge of computers as possible correlates of computer anxiety.

Math Anxiety and Sex

There has been speculation that the sex variable may correlate with computer anxiety. As Weinberg and English state,

> Part of this speculation is founded in the outmoded and sexist beliefs that women are somehow incapable of dealing with complex technology. Historical evidence, such as the invention of programming by Lady Lovelace in the 19th century, as well as contemporary observations in the job market, clearly refute this stereotype.

But the sex effect can also be suspected based on the negative socialization of women toward mathematics, science, and technology, and on the resulting production of anxieties. As Themes and others have discovered, the fears, attitudes, and alienation that result from this socialization process are strong correlates of math anxiety. Based on this rationale, then, math anxiety and sex have both been studied as possible correlates of computer anxiety. Weinberg and English found a correlation of only $-.0264$ between computer anxiety and sex, but a correlation of $.1225$ between math anxiety and computer anxiety. Yet Raub (1981) found the relationship between computer anxiety and sex so strong that she ran separate regressions for males and females. Her correlation between math anxiety and computer anxiety was on the order of $.30$ ($p < .05$) for both men and women.

Age

Age has been proposed as a correlate because of the belief that computer literacy is inversely related to age. Also, younger people are generally regarded to be more flexible attitudinally. Yet Weinberg and English found a correlation between age and computer anxiety of only .0067 that was only significant at the .444 level. Raub excluded age from her multiple regression analysis because the age data violated the linearity assumption. Both of these studies were inadequate in their treatment of age as a possible correlate because of the highly restricted range of ages in the samples.

Trait Anxiety

Themes (1982) and others (Betz, 1978; Rounds and Hendel, 1980) have found that trait anxiety is a significant correlate of math anxiety. For this reason, trait anxiety has been studied as a possible correlate of computer anxiety. The reasoning is that high trait-anxious individuals can be expected to exhibit state-anxious elevations such as computer anxiety more frequently than low trait-anxious individuals, as shown by Naylor and Guadry (1973). Weinberg and English did not study trait anxiety, but Raub found a .32 correlation ($p <$ .001) in males between trait anxiety and computer anxiety. Raub measured trait anxiety using the trait portion of the State Trait Anxiety Inventory (Spielberger, Gorsuch, and Lushene, 1970), a 20-item four-point Likert scale. Test-retest reliability for this instrument has been shown to be as high as .88 (Raub, 1981), and construct validity has been established by correlations with other methods of trait anxiety including the IPAT Anxiety Scale (Cattell and Scheier, 1963), the Taylor Manifest Anxiety Scale (Taylor, 1953), and the Zuckerman Affect Adjective Checklist (AACL) (Zuckerman, 1960).

Knowledge of Computers

Sandberg-Diment (1982) writes that "Computers are by their very nature intimidating to the uninitiated." This remark is suggestive of the theme throughout the computer anxiety literature that knowledge about computers and computer anxiety are likely to be inversely correlated. Knowledge coupled with successful experience ought to produce a successful attitude toward computers. Weinberg and English used an interview technique to assess level of training and found, surprisingly, no significant correlation. Raub however, found a significant correlation between computer experience and computer anxiety of –.43 in females and –.47 in males. Level of computer experience was measured in the Raub study using subjective questions that requested respondents to assess their computer knowledge. This is a questionable technique because it lacks objectivity and fails to make a clear distinction between knowledge and experience.

    The validity of most of these proposed correlates of computer anxiety has been at least partly confirmed by the preliminary studies reported here. These correlates however, fail to describe the psychological processes underlying computer anxiety. The present study will attempt to address these psychological questions.

Psychological Factors Related to Computer Anxiety

Part of this study is exploratory in nature in that it investigates whether there is any basis for inclusion of psychological variables as correlates of computer anxiety.

Locus of Control

As discussed in chapter 1, people can be classified as either internal or external types based on the psychological variable locus of control. The two types view themselves and their interactions with the world in very different ways. Internal types consider the forces that control their lives to be located within themselves. They believe that events depend entirely upon their own behavior. External types consider the forces that control their lives to be located outside themselves, and believe that luck, chance, fate, and powerful others are in control of their destiny. External locus of control is sometimes referred to as "learned helplessness" (Themes, 1982).

As DeSanctis (1982) reports, internals have greater motivation and have been shown to expend more effort, resources, and time in making decisions than externals (Elkins and Cochran, 1978). Rotter (1966) states that internals are likely to be more overt in striving for achievement. Broedling (1975) finds that as employees internals are more motivated to work and perform better than externals. And Lefcourt (1972) and Phares (1976) discover that internals engage in greater information search activity. They have also been shown to request more information than externals (Zmud, 1980), leading DeSanctis to speculate that they will tend to use a computerized decision support system more than will externals. DeSanctis's 1982 research confirms this speculation.

As Phares reports, a majority of studies find no significant sex effect in locus of control, but Barnett and Baruch (1978) find that women who achieve highly in mathematics tend to attribute their success to luck, suggesting that such women are probably external types.

Rosenman et al. (1970) studied the relationships among personality, anxiety, and stress. They identified Type A and Type B basic personality types. Type A people are hard driving, persistent, involved in work, oriented toward leadership and achievement, and have a sense of time urgency. These characteristics resemble those of internal locus of control types. The researchers found that Type A people are more anxiety-prone because of the hard-driving nature of their personality. Thus, it is reasonable to say that internal locus of control individuals, since they resemble Type A personalities, would tend toward high trait anxiety. But this conflicts with the speculation that internals would be less prone to computer anxiety because of their innate confidence in their ability to master challenges. Since the theoretical background is confusing and conflicting, research is needed to investigate the link (if any) between locus of control and computer anxiety.

Lazarus (1966) provides additional justification for inclusion of locus of control as a possible correlate of anxiety. He models the process as threat → appraisal → coping. A stressful situation presents a threat, the nature of the threat is appraised by the individual, with anxiety being created in the process, then the individual develops a defense scheme for coping with the threat. Lazarus states that a major determinant of whether the threat is appraised as dangerous or not so dangerous is the individual's "general belief about transactions with the environment." Internal locus of control types are better equipped psychologically to handle threats and can thus be expected to be less anxious in a threatening situation.

Cognitive Style

An individual's cognitive style is "the strategy or group of strategies that he or she typically adopts in approaching the solving of a wide variety of problem situations" (Shouksmith, 1970).

Mason and Mitroff (1973) suggest the inclusion of cognitive style in management information system (MIS) studies that seek to understand the cognitive processes underlying computer and information system usage. They note that much of the previous research has assumed "one underlying psychological type."

There is some MIS research that implies that attitudes of decision makers toward computers are dependent upon cognitive style, as reported by DeSanctis (1982). Cognitive style can be measured along a scale from analytic to heuristic. Analytic types have been found to have more positive expectations about the usefulness of a computer-based information system. High analytic types have also been found to perceive information systems as useful in decision making, because such people have an ability to impose structure on a disorganized set of facts (Witkin et al., 1971). Analytic decision makers are characterized by their tendency to look at details, while heuristic types tend to take an overall view (Lucas, 1981). Barkin found that analytic types tend to select a greater amount of information than heuristics in an experimental setting (Dickson, Senn, and Chervany, 1977). And Lusk and Kersnick (1979) discovered that in a highly structured environment analytic types performed much better than heuristics. All of these studies imply that the structure, quantity of information, and details preferred by analytics would attract them to computers. This suggests in turn that analytic types would have a lower incidence of computer anxiety simply because the kind of thinking required for successful interaction with a computer is the kind of thinking that analytics naturally prefer.

Treating Computer Anxiety

Literature on the treatment of computer anxiety is even more sparse than that on the origins and correlates of the phenomenon. This sparse literature was reviewed in chapter 1. Literature on treatment of the related phenomenon of math anxiety was reviewed earlier in the present chapter. Treatment techniques for both computer anxiety and math anxiety center around correcting the problem by giving knowledge or experience or a combination of the two. For example, Raub (1981) reports that the American Management Association sponsors a conference on computer anxiety that directly addresses computer technology and applications in business. The conference is designed to give middle managers who are not computer-literate sufficient background to make more efficient use of computing resources.

Raub argues that such training courses might not be particularly effective if given over a short period of time. Based on clinical interviews with students suffering very high computer anxiety, she has extended Erickson's (1963) stage theory of human development to develop a stage theory of computer anxiety. The theory posits that computer anxiety consists of a heterogeneous set of fears that evolve along an assimilation/accommodation continuum. The five stages are computer alienation, recognized impact on society, impact on personal life, computer accommodation, and assimilation of computer knowledge. Briefly, the theory models the computer anxiety treatment process as requiring a classic unfreezing, change, and refreezing sequence of steps. The Raub theory obviously implies that, to be effective, the treatment for computer anxiety must be given over an extended period of time. This is consistent with Weinberg's view (James, 1982) that treating computer anxiety requires "ever-increasing exposure to the source of the terror." These theories are tested in the pre-post portion of the present study.

3

Design and Methodology

The study is actually two investigations in one. Component I, the correlates study, was a field study that employed a questionnaire to sample a number of managers and executives to determine their attitudes toward using microcomputers in management, the incidence of computer anxiety, and the correlates of computer anxiety in managers. Component II, the pre-post study, consisted of a controlled laboratory experiment to determine whether a brief training session on microcomputers and microcomputer-based management software could significantly improve managers' attitudes toward microcomputers, reduce their computer anxiety, or both.

Mechanically, the two components of the study were performed independently, but their results complement each other in increased understanding of the computer anxiety phenomenon and of managers' attitudes toward microcomputers.

Research Questions

The research questions of the study that appear in chapter 1 are reproduced here for convenience. The correlates study addresses the first two questions, and the pre-post study addresses the remainder of the questions.

1. What are managers' attitudes toward the usefulness of micro-computers as management tools? Can any factors be discovered that are significantly correlated with these attitudes?
2. To what degree do managers suffer from computer anxiety? Can any factors be discovered that are significantly correlated with computer anxiety in managers?
3. Can managers' attitudes toward the usefulness of microcomputers as management tools be changed significantly by a brief training session on microcomputers? What kinds of individuals are most susceptible to attitude change?

4. Does high computer anxiety appear to present a barrier to managers' attitude change as a result of a training session?
5. Are managers' levels of computer anxiety after a training session significantly different than before the training session?

These research questions are stated in relatively general terms. The questions lead, in turn, to a number of more specific hypotheses that are tested using the data that the study generated.

Hypotheses

The hypotheses are uniquely labeled using letters. Additionally, each hypothesis is labeled to indicate the component of the study and the research question with which it is associated. The first field in the parentheses following each hypothesis will contain "F" or "P-P" for the field or pre-post component, and the second field indicates the research question that the hypothesis addresses.

Hypothesis A (F,1)
H_o: There will be no significant correlation between a manager's attitude toward his or her using microcomputers in management and the manager's computer anxiety.
H_a: Managers with high computer anxiety will have less favorable attitudes toward using microcomputers.

Hypothesis B (F,1)
H_o: There will be no significant correlation between a manager's attitude toward his or her using microcomputers in management and the manager's assessment of the possible impact of computers on society.
H_a: Managers with less favorable assessments of the possible impact of computers on society will have less favorable attitudes toward using microcomputers.

Hypothesis C (F,1)
H_o: There will be no significant correlation between a manager's attitude toward his or her using microcomputers in management and the manager's math anxiety.
H_a: Managers with high math anxiety will have less favorable attitudes toward using microcomputers.

Hypothesis D (F,1)

H_o: There will be no significant correlation between a manager's attitude toward his or her using microcomputers in management and the manager's age.

H_a: Older managers will have less favorable attitudes toward using microcomputers.

Hypothesis E (F,1)

H_o: There will be no significant difference in managers' attitudes toward using microcomputers in management between men and women managers.

H_a: Women managers will have less favorable attitudes toward using microcomputers.

Hypothesis F (F,1)

H_o: There will be no significant correlation between a manager's attitude toward his or her using microcomputers in management and the manager's level of general computer knowledge.

H_a: Managers with low general computer knowledge will have less favorable attitudes toward using microcomputers.

Hypothesis G (F,1)

H_o: There will be no significant correlation between a manager's attitude toward his or her using microcomputers in management and the manager's level of general computer experience.

H_a: Managers with less general computer experience will have less favorable attitudes toward using microcomputers.

Hypothesis H (F,1)

H_o: There will be no significant correlation between a manager's attitude toward his or her using microcomputers in management and the manager's level of trait anxiety.

H_a: Managers with high trait anxiety will have less favorable attitudes toward using microcomputers.

Hypothesis I (F,1)

H_o: There will be no significant correlation between managers' attitudes toward using microcomputers in management and their scores on the internal/external locus of control instrument.

H_a: External locus of control managers will have less favorable attitudes toward using microcomputers.

Hypothesis J (F,1)

H$_o$: There will be no significant correlation between managers' attitudes toward using microcomputers in management and their scores on the cognitive style instrument.

H$_a$: Heuristic cognitive style managers will have less favorable attitudes toward using microcomputers.

The next nine hypotheses are identical in form to those preceding except that in each hypothesis the manager's attitudes toward his or her using microcomputers in management variable is replaced by the computer anxiety variable. Table 1 lists equivalencies for hypotheses K through S, in lieu of restating all nine hypotheses in long form.

Hypothesis T (P-P,3)

H$_o$: There will be no significant change in managers' attitudes toward their using microcomputers in management as a result of a brief training session on microcomputers and microcomputer-based management software.

H$_a$: The managers will have a significantly more favorable attitude toward using microcomputers after the training session.

There are two additional subhypotheses related to Hypothesis T that will be tested if the null hypothesis of T is rejected.

Hypothesis T' (P-P,3)

H$_o$: There will be no significant difference between the attitude change of internal locus of control managers versus external locus of control managers.

H$_a$: Internal locus of control managers will experience significantly more improvement in attitude than external locus of control managers.

Hypothesis T" (P-P,3)

H$_o$: There will be no significant difference between the attitude change of analytical cognitive style managers versus heuristic cognitive style managers.

H$_a$: Analytical cognitive style managers will experience significantly more improvement in attitude than heuristic cognitive style managers.

Hypothesis U (P-P,5)

This hypothesis is identical to Hypothesis T except that the phrase "managers' attitudes toward their using microcomputers

Table 1. Table of Hypothesis Equivalencies

Hypothesis	Parallels Hypothesis
K (F,2)	B (F,1)
L (F,2)	C (F,1)
M (F,2)	D (F,1)
N (F,2)	E (F,1)
O (F,2)	F (F,1)
P (F,2)	G (F,1)
Q (F,2)	H (F,1)
R (F,2)	I (F,1)
S (F,2)	J (F,1)

in management" in the null hypothesis should be replaced by "managers' level of computer anxiety." The microcomputer attitude variable in the alternate hypotheses should be replaced by the level of computer anxiety variable.

Hypothesis V (P-P,4)

H_o: There is no significant difference in the treatment group between managers with high and low computer anxiety in the amount of attitude change that results from the training course on microcomputers.

H_a: High computer anxiety managers experience significantly less attitude improvement from the training course than do managers with low pretreatment anxiety.

All of the above hypotheses have their foundation in the conceptual framework and literature review of the preceding chapters. Although they are stated in true null hypothesis form, the alternate hypotheses contain the expectations of the results as suggested by the literature and the theory.

Measurement Instruments

This section lists the variables involved in both components of the study and identifies and describes the various instruments used to measure these variables. Reliability data and some pretest results are included.

Variables

Table 2 lists the variables in the study for which measurement instruments were used. The table indicates to which of the parts of the study each variable pertains and gives its polar extremes. The balance of this section describes the measurement techniques used for each of the variables.

Attitude toward Microcomputers

This variable describes a particular manager's attitude toward his or her personally using a microcomputer for assistance in management tasks. This is distinct from a manager's attitude toward microcomputers in general, because it has been widely reported that many managers who recognize the value of microcomputers and who support and encourage their subordinates' use of "micros" are very uncomfortable with the idea of using microcomputers themselves (Klein, 1983). The object is to measure this attitude along an "Unfavorable–Favorable" scale. No such instrument exists, so one was developed as part of the pilot study, as described below.

Development of the attitude toward microcomputers instrument. The attitude toward microcomputers instrument was developed following Likert's (1961) classic procedure, the steps being development of an item pool, administration of the item pool to a group of managers, factor analysis of the results, and final construction of an instrument.

Creating the item pool. On June 17, 1983, a group of Kent State Executive MBA (EMBA) students (N = 23) were asked to complete the questionnaire shown in appendix A. The questionnaire asked the respondents to indicate whether they were managers or "nonmanagement professionals" and to respond to the following question.

> What do you see as the major advantages and disadvantages of your personally using a microcomputer such as the Apple II, TRS-80, IBM PC, etc. in your present position?

The 18 questionnaires that remained, after eliminating those from nonmanagement professionals, were analyzed by the author, and a list of 36 advantages and 39 disadvantages of microcomputer use was compiled. These expressed concerns were combined with a group of 6 other microcomputer concerns that appear frequently in articles on the topic, and the resulting 81 items were reworded so that they could be responded to in Agree–Disagree terms. The questionnaire generated from the 81-item pool appears in appendix B.

Table 2. Variables for Which Measurement Instruments Were Used

Variable	Used Component:	Polar Extremes
Attitude toward microcomputer use	F, P-P	Unfavorable - Favorable
Computer anxiety	F, P-P	Low - High
Impact of computers on society	F	Unfavorable - Favorable
Math anxiety	F	Low - High
Locus of control	F, P-P	Internal - External
Cognitive style	F, P-P	Heuristic - Analytical
Trait anxiety	F	Low - High
Computer knowledge	F	Low - High
Computer experience	F	Limited - Extensive

The fact that EMBA students voluntarily elect to spend the time and effort to participate in graduate business study refutes any claim that they are a representative sample of the overall population of managers. But for the purpose of building a microcomputer attitudes item pool, this group of managers is nearly ideal because they are more likely to be aware of the existence of microcomputer technology and of the advantages and disadvantages of its use than are managers at large. Thus the 81 items in the present item pool represent a fairly complete list of microcomputer concerns, compiled from the collective wisdom and experience of a group of well-educated managers, and the fact that the respondents were not randomly selected does not seriously detract from the usefulness of the results.

Administration of the questionnaire. The questionnaire in appendix B was administered anonymously to the same group of EMBA students on June 24. This was done prior to the microcomputer training portion of the EMBA course so that the results of the item pool administration would not be affected. The class was told only that the questionnaire was being given in connection with Graduate School of Management research, and that their responses and opinions would be highly valued. As before, the questionnaires from nonmanagement professionals were excluded, and the remaining questionnaires (N = 18) were subjected to a factor analysis.

Factor analysis. The purpose of the factor analysis was to lend construct validity to the microcomputer attitudes instrument by discovering whether any underlying patterns to the responses could be found that would permit a reduction in the number of items in the questionnaire.

Principal factoring (without iterations) and the varimax rotation method were used (SPSS procedure FACTOR). Items 79 and 81 of the item pool questionnaire (see appendix B) were excluded from the factor analysis. These items pertain to the microcomputer attitudes of managers' organizations rather than to the individual managers. The factor analysis identified six factors that each accounted for more than 5% of the total variance, as shown in table 3. Eleven other factors were identified, each of which accounted for a very small percentage of the total variance, giving a total explained variance of 100%.

The varimax rotated factor matrix was then studied in an effort to understand and name the six significant factors. Thirty-three of the 81 items loaded greater than $|.4|$ on factor 1. For example, the rotated factor loadings for items 9, 11, 15, and 23 were .56, .69, .91, and .69, respectively. These four items were:

9. A microcomputer would give me more timely access to needed information.
11. A microcomputer could provide me with information in a form exactly tailored to my needs.
15. Using a microcomputer, I could create my own personal data base of important information.
23. Using a microcomputer could provide me with information that would lead to better decisions.

The obvious theme running through these, and nearly all of the other items that loaded heavily on this factor, was one of improved information through improved access. Hence factor 1 was named "Improved access to information." This particular factor is an important component of managers' overall attitudes toward microcomputers, accounting for slightly more than one-third of the total variance in the factor analysis.

Factors 2 through 6 were named using a similar procedure. Table 4 gives the names for all six factors and a count of the number of items loading greater than $|.4|$ on each. Factor 2 reflects the managers' concern that the time required to use microcomputers (inputting data, programming) might offset any advantages of their use. Factor 3 expresses concern that the speed and storage capabilities of microcomputers may be insufficient to give them real-world usefulness. Factor 4 loaded on items such as "I wouldn't use a microcomputer because this would be clerical in nature." This shows a concern with maintenance of managerial image. Factor 5 loaded on a group of items that revealed fears that micros are more trouble than they are worth. Factor 6 is self-explanatory from its name. All six of these factors are concerns that appear repeatedly in the business literature.

The size of the management group used to develop these results (N = 18) is small, but the main concern in the validity of factor analysis is that a large number of significant items can be found for each factor, and that was clearly the case here. The factor loadings by item appear in appendix C.

Table 3. Summarized Factor Analysis Results

Factor	Eigenvalue	Percent of Variance	Cumulative Variance
1	28.58	36.2	36.2
2	8.42	10.7	46.9
3	5.58	7.1	54.0
4	4.95	6.3	60.3
5	4.74	6.0	66.3
6	4.13	5.2	71.5

Table 4. Named Factors

Factor	Factor Name	Items Loading > $\mid .4 \mid$
1	Improved access to information	35
2	Time to use	24
3	Lack of capability	24
4	Using microcomputer not consistent with normal managerial tasks	10
5	More trouble and expense than they're worth	5
6	Problems of proliferation of microcomputers and the resulting incompatibilities of hardware, software, and data	4

Development of the finalized instrument. The final version of the attitudes toward microcomputers instrument was constructed by selecting four items from those items that loaded heavily on each of the six factors, giving a total of 24 questions. The selections were based on a combination of high loadings and a subjective evaluation of the degree to which the selected items were representative of the main theme of each factor. The 24 items ultimately selected from the 81-item pool were: 9, 11, 15, and 23 for factor 1; 2, 4, 8, and 28 for factor 2; 52, 64, 68, and 72 for factor 3; 12, 32, 38, and 71 for factor 4; 16, 20, 24, and 80 for factor 5; and 50, 54, 61, and 62 for factor 6. Item 50 was chosen in preference to item 41, which had a higher loading, because it was more appropriate to the obvious theme of factor 6. The order of these 24 items was scrambled, and they appear as questions 1 through 24 of the final questionnaire in appendix D.

Construct validity for the attitudes toward microcomputers instrument was established, to the extent possible, by the preceding factor analysis. The reliability of this new instrument was determined using data from the field study (see chapter 4).

Computer Anxiety

Raub (1981) has developed an instrument to measure computer attitudes. Her factor analysis of the results of administering this instrument clearly identified three factors: an appreciation of computers and a desire to learn more about them, computer usage anxiety, and fears about the computer's possible negative impact on society. The ten items that Raub used to measure the second of the above factors, computer usage anxiety, will be used in the present study. There are no other measures of computer anxiety that can be used to check rigorously the construct validity of Raub's instrument, but the factor analysis coupled with her extensive clinical interviews of respondents to the questionnaire lend considerable validity to the instrument. Raub does not report any reliability data. The present study checks the reliability of the computer anxiety instrument in pretest and post hoc tests (discussed later in this chapter and in chapter 4). Questions 25 through 34 of the questionnaire in appendix D make up the computer anxiety instrument.

Impact of Computers on Society

This variable was measured using the questions associated with the third factor of Raub's questionnaire, as discussed above. Construct validity and reliability are similar to the computer anxiety instrument. Questions 35 through 42 of the questionnaire in appendix D were used to assess this variable.

Math Anxiety

Math anxiety was measured using Fennema and Sherman's well-established (1976) instrument. Construct validity has been checked by comparison with other math anxiety instruments, and Betz (1978) reports a reliability of .92 using the split-half method. Questions 43 through 54 of the appendix D questionnaire make up the math anxiety instrument.

Locus of Control

Rotter (1966) developed the classic instrument for measurement of locus of control. The instrument has been criticized, however, because of its length (29 items) and because the content themes of some of the items dwell on school-related themes (Valecha and Ostrom, 1974). Valecha and Ostrom developed a shortened version of Rotter's instrument that corrects these problems, and their instrument was used in the present study. The shortened instrument comprises 11 items, none of which has any school-related content. Construct validity has been carefully established, as reported in the foregoing reference, and reliability is reported as .62 (N = 3,694) using Cronbach's alpha. Questions 55 through 65 of the questionnaire in appendix D measure the respondent's locus of control. Scoring was done as specified in the reference.

Cognitive Style

As noted in chapter 2, cognitive style is most often assessed using the Group Embedded Figures Test (Witkin et al., 1971). This test is quite time-consuming, however, and must be carefully administered. The instrument does not lend itself to a questionnaire study. Barkin (1974) has developed a cognitive style instrument that is more suitable for a study of this sort and that has good construct validity. Barkin reports a reliability of .85 (N = 204) using the Kuder-Richardson 20 method. Items 66 through 82 of the questionnaire in appendix D make up the cognitive style instrument.

Trait Anxiety

Spielberger, Gorsuch, and Lushene (1970) have developed a 20-item trait anxiety instrument, the construct validity of which has been solidly established by correlations with other measures of trait anxiety, as reported in chapter 2. Test-retest reliability of this instrument has been shown to be as high as .88 (Raub, 1981). The Spielberger, Gorsuch, and Lushene instrument is questions 83 through 102 of the appendix D questionnaire.

Computer Knowledge

Measurement of this variable does not require a psychometric instrument, per se, but simply a brief objective test (questions 103 through 112, appendix D). The goal is to distinguish between people with virtually no computer knowledge and those with relatively extensive knowledge. This ten-item test, developed by the author, contains questions from the three broad areas of hardware (questions 103, 104, 110), software (questions 106, 108, 109, 112), and systems (questions 105, 107, 111). Within each of these groups, there are trivially easy questions and questions that require advanced and current knowledge. The construct validity of the test is obvious from the wording of the questions. Reliability of this test was checked using a pretest and post hoc analysis, as will be described later.

Computer Experience

This is a demographic variable. Questions 113 through 118 of the questionnaire (appendix D) measure experience in computing by considering both the length and breadth of experience. A composite experience score is then calculated for each respondent.

Table 5 summarizes the measurement instruments just described.

The Consolidated Questionnaire Battery

The consolidated questionnaire battery, entitled "Computer Attitudes Survey," (appendix D) comprises a set of instructions, all of the questions associated with the measurement instruments discussed above, and a set of demographic questions that were used to characterize the sample of managers that responded to the questionnaire.

Pilot Test of Questionnaire Administration Procedures

To test the readability and understandability of the instructions, and to get an estimate of the administration time, a draft of the consolidated questionnaire battery was given to a class of Kent State University undergraduate students ($N= 14$) on August 3, 1983. The average completion time was 20.6 minutes, with $\sigma = 2.4$ minutes. Minimum and maximum completion times were 18 and 25 minutes. The students were placed under no time pressure to complete the questionnaire, and the administration was done at the beginning of the class period rather than at the end when students are anxious to leave.

The students were interviewed collectively afterward, and they made no comments with regard to vague or misleading instructions.

No use will be made of the results other than those given above, as this was simply a pilot test of the mechanical administration procedures for the questionnaire.

Pilot Test to Collect Reliability Data

No prior reliability data were available on the attitudes toward microcomputers, computer anxiety, impact of computers on society, or computer knowledge instruments. It would not be reasonable to administer the attitudes toward microcomputers questions to undergraduate business students and expect to get an accurate assessment of the reliability of this instrument as it applies to managers. Meaningful responses to the questions in

Table 5. Summary of Measurement Techniques

Variable	Instrument
Attitude toward microcomputers	New instrument developed by Howard
Computer anxiety	Raub (1981)
Impact of computers on society	Raub (1981)
Math anxiety	Fennema and Sherman (1976)
Locus of control	Valecha and Ostrom (1974)
Cognitive style	Barkin (1974)
Trait anxiety	Spielberger et al. (1970)
Computer knowledge	New test by Howard
Computer experience	New scale by Howard

this instrument require a base of real-world management experience. It would, however, be reasonable to use responses from undergraduate business students to obtain preliminary reliability estimates for the other three instruments.

The consolidated questionnaire battery was administered anonymously to 91 undergraduate business students on September 29, 1983. The respondents were placed under no time pressure and were told to ignore the first 24 questions (the attitudes toward microcomputer questions). A total of 83 usable questionnaires were obtained. Internal consistency was calculated for the computer anxiety, impact of computers on society, and computer knowledge instruments using the split-half method. Results are shown in table 6.

The reliabilities for the computer anxiety and societal impact instruments are well in line with the reliabilities of most well-established psychometric instruments. The computer knowledge test was intentionally constructed with a mix of easy and difficult questions, and there were three easy and two hard questions in the first split half used for the reliability calculations and vice versa in the other half. This would downwardly bias the results. Considering this inherent understatement in the computer knowledge reliability estimate, a value of .60 is respectable.

Design and Method: Correlates Study

The objective of the correlates study was to collect data that can be used to test all of the hypotheses connected with component I—the field study of the correlates of computer anxiety and of managers' attitudes toward microcomputers.

Table 6.   Reliability Estimates from the Pilot Test

Instrument	Split-Half Reliability
Computer anxiety	.87 (N = 83)
Impact of computers on society	.74 (N = 83)
Computer knowledge	.60 (N = 81)

Design

Data for the correlates study were collected by administering the consolidated questionnaire battery to a randomly selected group of managers. The resulting data were then analyzed and used to test the field study hypotheses using the statistical techniques described in chapter 4. This exploratory study seeks only to determine whether any of the variables are significantly correlated. It will remain the task of a future study to address issues of causality.

Sample and Procedure

Students in the fall 1983 MBA and EMBA classes at Kent State University (KSU) were used to help select a random sample of managers from northeastern Ohio industry to whom the consolidated questionnaire battery would be given. Each of the approximately 30 participating students was given a packet containing ten questionnaires and an instruction sheet. The instructions asked the student to distribute the questionnaires to ten randomly selected management level people at his or her place of employment. Each of the instruction sheets was accompanied by a different computer-generated list of ten random letters of the alphabet with no duplicates. The student was asked to deliver a questionnaire to the first person in the corporate directory or telephone book whose last name began with each of the ten letters. If the first person in the listings for that letter was not a manager or was inaccessible to the student, if the student preferred for political reasons not to involve that person, or if the person refused to complete the questionnaire, then the student was asked to proceed alphabetically down the corporate list within that letter until a cooperating manager was found. As an incentive to participation, respondents were offered optional feedback, which included a brief synopsis of the purpose of the study and a computer-generated score sheet. The ten questionnaires were distributed in this way and then collected by the MBA and EMBA students to be returned to KSU. The students themselves did not complete questionnaires because they are not, as noted earlier, representative of the population of managers as a whole. The MBA and EMBA students acted simply as couriers, conveying the questionnaires to the respondents and returning them when complete.

Of the approximately 30 students who accepted packets, 16 actually distributed the questionnaires, and a total of 111 usable questionnaires were returned. This yields a response rate of 111/160 or 69.4% and provides a sufficient number of responses to give very good statistical significance to the results.

This was obviously a sample of convenience, but it would be hard to argue that this convenient sample is not also a representative sample of managers from northeastern Ohio industry. More rigorously stated, however, the sample is a random group of managers from organizations having at least one employee who participates in the KSU MBA or EMBA program.

The data analysis and results appear in the next chapter.

Design and Method: Pre-Post Study

The objective of the pre-post portion of the study was to design and conduct an experiment that supports tests of hypotheses T, U, and V. These three hypotheses relate to research questions 3, 5, and 4, respectively.

Design

Figure 2 shows the overall design, which is the classic pretest-posttest control group design with random assignment to groups, as discussed by Winer (1971). This is essentially a two-factor design with "group" (treatment or control) as one factor and measurement "trial" (pretest or posttest) the other factor. The trial factor was not used, per se, in the present study because repeated measures ANOVA was not employed, as discussed in chapter 4. One additional factor, EMBA class, is involved in the analysis. This factor is not shown in figure 2 so as not to obscure the basic design. The role of this factor in the analysis is discussed in chapter 4. The advantages of factorial designs such as economy, sensitivity, experimental control, generality, and the detection of interactions are well established (Keppel, 1973). Random assignment of subjects to either the control group or the treatment group effectively controls for subject differences and for any systematic differences in the conditions of the experiment between the groups, as Keppel also notes.

The treatment group received the microcomputer training and the control group did not. Counterbalancing was used in the administration of the training. Both groups completed pretest and posttest questionnaires. This design arrangement is portrayed schematically in figure 3.

Figure 2. Generalized Design of the Pre-Post Study

			Factor B (Trials)	
			b_1	b_2
		Subject	Pretest	Posttest
a_1	Treatment Group	1	X_{111}	X_{121}
		2	X_{112}	X_{122}
		3	X_{113}	X_{123}
		4	X_{114}	X_{124}
a_2	Control Group	5	X_{215}	X_{225}
		6	X_{216}	X_{226}
		7	X_{217}	X_{227}
		8	X_{218}	X_{228}

Figure 3. Schematic Representation of the Experimental Design

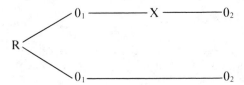

Sample and Procedure

The experimental subjects were students in two KSU EMBA classes. This immediately suggests limitations on the broad generalizability of the experimental results obtained, because managers who participate in the EMBA program are clearly not representative of the overall population of managers. It is important to realize, though, that the experiment seeks to measure *differential,* and not absolute effects. The interest is in the amount of *change* in such areas as computer anxiety and microcomputer attitudes that occurs as a result of the experimental treatment, and not in the absolute initial levels of these variables. It is recognized that the use of EMBA managers is a methodological limitation, but much less so than if the goal were to measure absolute levels of computer anxiety and microcomputer attitudes.

The experiment was conducted on each EMBA class on two separate days. Class was included as a factor in the analysis so that any systematic differences between the two EMBA classes would be discovered at the time of the analysis. The EMBA classes are intact, rather than randomly selected groups, but random selection within classes was employed.

Each EMBA class was given the Computer Attitudes Survey (appendix D), which constituted the pretest. Following completion of the pretest, the students were assigned randomly to three groups. (Assignment of students to groups had been done prior to the class session using a random number table and the class roster.) Half of each class constituted the control group. The remaining half was further subdivided into two treatment subgroups, one of which would receive first the microcomputer demonstration and then the hands-on experience, the other of which would receive these "treatments" in reverse order. Each student was given a card randomly selected from a deck of playing cards and asked to indicate the card received on both the pretest and posttest. This was done to assure correct pairing of the pretests and posttests while retaining respondents' anonymity. Then the treatment group was taken to the microcomputer laboratory while the control group remained in the classroom. The explanation for dividing the class was that the laboratory could not accommodate everyone at once, and that the second group would go to the laboratory in the second half of the class period.

An introductory lecture on the BASIC programming language was given to the control group. It is recognized that this was not the ideal scheme, but the experimental conditions did not permit a more neutral activity in the control group, as is discussed further in chapter 4.

Subdivision of the treatment group was done partly for practical reasons and partly for experimental design reasons. No attempt was made in the study to distinguish whether any effects of the treatment are separately due to either the demonstration or the hands-on phase of the treatment, but the order of the phases may be important. To cancel any effects of order, the counterbalancing design advocated by Keppel was employed. This arrangement was operationally simpler as well, because only about ten people needed to be in a position to view the demonstration. Also, the trainer giving the hands-on phase was able to supervise the instruction more effectively. Figure 4 shows the overall schedule of the class session.

Content of the demonstration phase was as shown in figure 5. The objective of this phase was to dazzle the managers with the impressive capabilities of freestanding microcomputers. The demonstration was conducted by the author in a seminar room adjacent to the microcomputer laboratory. The equipment complement was an IBM PC with 256K RAM and two disk drives, a monochrome monitor, a color monitor, a dot matrix graphics printer, and a Hewlett-Packard flatbed plotter. When the managers entered the room the plotter was in the final 3 minutes of producing a multicolor bar graph, a task that required a total of 18 minutes to complete. The managers were told that at the end of the session they would be shown the steps that were taken to initiate creation of the plot.

Figure 4.   Schedule of Activities for EMBA Class Sessions

Time for This Activity	Control Group Activity	Treatment Group Activity	Total Elapsed Time
00:05	Introduce session		00:05
00:30	Take pretest		00:35
00:05	Make group assignments and turn in pretests		00:40
00:10	BASIC programming lecture	Move to micro-computer lab	00:50
00:30		Demo/ Hands-on	01:20
00:30		Hands-on/ Demo	01:50
00:05		Return to class	01:55
00:10	Take posttest		02:05
00:10	Move to micro-computer lab	Break	02:15
00:30	Demo/ Hands-on phases	BASIC lecture	02:45
00:30	Hands-on/ Demo phases		03:15
	Class ends		

A brief presentation was given to insure that the managers fully appreciated the magnitude of the explosion of microcomputer use in business, and they were given a handout to read later that contained several recent articles on this theme.

The balance of the demonstration was done using Lotus 1-2-3, a high level, user-friendly business software package that currently is experiencing great commercial success. A small spreadsheet was shown first to explain the principles and mechanics behind the spreadsheet concept. The bulk of the demonstration however, centered around a very large database that contained historical and projected data for the population, effective buying income, and retail sales for each county in the state of Idaho. This spreadsheet contained on the order of 3,500 data items. The rationale was to show the power of the

Figure 5.   Content of the Demonstration Phase

1.   Brief summary of the rate of growth of   5 min.
      microcomputer usage in business, with an
      accompanying handout to be read later

2.   Simple spreadsheet—MDC Corporation   5 min.
      Consolidated Balance Sheet

3.   Very large spreadsheet—Idaho demographics
      and market potential database

      A.   Show magnitude and mechanics   5 min.
            of spreadsheet
      B.   Demonstrate database queries   5 min.
      C.   Display a color graph   2 min.
      D.   Illustrate plotting of a color graph   3 min.

4.   Questions and discussion   5 min.

microcomputer to handle business data on a realistically large scale as
opposed to an artificially small textbook or classroom example. Each
manager received a handout summarizing the detailed content of the
demonstration.

Concurrent with this demonstration, the other half of the treatment
group was receiving hands-on training in the microcomputer laboratory.
Each manager was seated at an IBM PC and given both a blank diskette and a
diskette containing the operating system and demonstration software. The
trainer led the tutorial on bringing up the machine, executing simple DOS
(Disk-Based Operating System) commands such as DISKCOPY, basic
editing, and the mechanics of entering and running interpretive BASIC
programs. The group was small enough to allow the trainer to give personal
attention to each of the managers.

After 30 minutes, the managers in the two treatment subgroups swapped
rooms, and the demonstration and hands-on phases were repeated. At the
completion of this latter period, all of the treatment group managers were
asked to complete a posttest questionnaire that consisted of the computer
anxiety and attitudes toward microcomputers instruments. Concurrently, the
control group managers were completing this same posttest in the classroom.
At this point the experiment was complete, but the class period was not. After

a break the control group was given the two-phased microcomputer training and demonstration session, and the treatment group received the introductory lecture on the BASIC programming language.

As noted before, this entire experimental procedure was done twice, once for each of the two participating EMBA classes, on October 21 and October 29, 1983.

Chapter 4 discusses the analysis techniques and separately presents the results of the correlates study and the laboratory study.

4

Analysis and Results

This chapter describes the analysis techniques employed and presents the results of the data analysis. The correlates study and the laboratory study are discussed separately. For readers who wish to avoid excessive detail, a concise summary of the results appears at the end of the chapter.

Correlates Study

Variables

Table 7 describes the variables used in the correlates study. The "optimistic classification" of each variable is based on a loose interpretation of the rules for levels of measurement, while the "pessimistic classification" reflects a stricter interpretation of the statistical definitions. The techniques and instruments used to measure the variables in this table were described in chapter 3.

It is not uncommon in psychological and behavioral research to treat the scores produced by psychometric instruments as interval data. This is an optimistic, liberal view of the data. In this view, a person with a trait anxiety score of 44 is considered exactly one "unit" more trait anxious than a person with a score of 43, and two units more trait anxious than someone scoring 42. Kleinbaum and Kupper (1978) state, though, that "To be interval, a variable must have some sort of standard or well-accepted physical unit of measurement." Height, weight, and blood pressure are given as examples of interval data. Thus, it is not strictly correct to consider psychometric data as interval data because there is no physical unit of measurement. Some social science methodology experts argue that statistical analysis procedures such as regression and Pearson correlations may be validly used on ordinal data, rather than on interval data, as required by the assumptions of these procedures. But this practice can lead to erroneous conclusions. Accordingly, the present study will take a conservative approach, treating the variables according to their pessimistic classifications as given in table 7.

Table 7. Characteristics of Variables in the Correlates Study

Variable Name	Symbol	Polar Extremes	Range of Numerical Scores	Optimistic Classification	Pessimistic Classification
Attitude toward microcomputers	MCRATT	Unfavorable – Favorable	0 – 96	Interval	Ordinal
Attitude – Factor 1	MCRAT1	Unfavorable – Favorable	0 – 16	Interval	Ordinal
Attitude – Factor 2	MCRAT2	Unfavorable – Favorable	0 – 16	Interval	Ordinal
Attitude – Factor 3	MCRAT3	Unfavorable – Favorable	0 – 16	Interval	Ordinal
Attitude – Factor 4	MCRAT4	Unfavorable – Favorable	0 – 16	Interval	Ordinal
Attitude – Factor 5	MCRAT5	Unfavorable – Favorable	0 – 16	Interval	Ordinal
Attitude – Factor 6	MCRAT6	Unfavorable – Favorable	0 – 16	Interval	Ordinal
Computer anxiety	CMPANX	Low – High	0 – 40	Interval	Ordinal
Impact of computers on society	SOCIMP	Unfavorable – Favorable	0 – 32	Interval	Ordinal
Math anxiety	MTHANX	Low – High	0 – 48	Interval	Ordinal
Locus of control	LOCCTL	Internal – External	11 – 44	Interval	Ordinal
Cognitive style	COGSTL	Heuristic – Analytical	0 – 17	Interval	Ordinal
Trait anxiety	TRTANX	Low – High	0 – 60	Interval	Ordinal
Computer knowledge	CMPKNW	Low – High	0 – 10	Interval	Ordinal
Computer experience	CMPEXP	Limited – Extensive	0 – 18	Interval	Ordinal
Years of work experience	YRSEXP	N/A	(*)	Ratio	Ratio
Manager's age	AGE	N/A	(*)	Ratio	Ratio
Manager's sex	SEX	N/A	1=M,2=F	Nominal	Nominal

*The range of these data will be determined by the data as they are received.

Except for age, sex, and years of experience, this means that all the variables in the correlates study are ordinal. Thus a person with a trait anxiety score of 44 is considered to have a higher level of trait anxiety than a person scoring 43, and the person scoring 43 is in turn more trait anxious than a person with a score of 42. Ordinal data do not attempt to quantify the differences between scores; they only specify order. Adoption of the ordinality assumption and of proper analysis procedures for ordinal data will, in the present study, produce conclusions that are technically correct and statistically conservative.

Descriptive Statistics

Table 8 summarizes the descriptive statistics for all of the variables in the correlates study except sex. These values were calculated from the sample of 111 participating managers. SPSS procedure FREQUENCIES was used.

The sample contained 90 male, 19 female managers, and 2 who did not indicate their sex. With an average age of approximately 38 years and an average span of experience of about 17 years, the sample obviously represents a group of experienced managers. Also, the span of ages (24 years to 60 years) and of years of experience (2 to 40) suggests that the sample captures a broad cross section of the population of managers.

The managers in the sample have a notably positive attitude toward the usefulness of microcomputers in management. With possible scores on each of the six attitude factors of 0 (unfavorable attitude) to 16 (favorable attitude), the averages on five of the six factors were all approximately 12. (See table 4 for identification of the six factors.) For factor 6, the average attitude score was 9.05. While this last score reflects a favorable attitude, it does indicate a modest degree of concern among the managers about possible problems of proliferation of microcomputers and the resulting incompatibilities of hardware, software, and data. With respect to the other five factors, the managers seem to feel strongly that microcomputers can provide improved access to information, that the time required to use them is reasonable, that they possess sufficient computational and storage capabilities to make them useful in full-scale, real-world management applications, that their use will not damage the executive image, and that microcomputers are well worth the trouble and expense. There are, of course, no norms for these attitude scores because this was the first use of the attitudes toward microcomputers instrument. But the descriptive statistics in table 8 are strongly suggestive of the above general conclusions.

One of the many objectives of the study was to gain some sense of the incidence of computer anxiety in managers. It is difficult to make an informed judgment on this issue from the table 8 data because of, again, the lack of norms. The question is which numerical scores should be interpreted as

Table 8.   Descriptive Statistics from the Correlates Study (N = 111)

Variable Symbol	Minimum Value	Maximum Value	Mean	Standard Deviation
MCRATT	28	93	69.03	10.58
MCRAT1	3	16	11.54	2.10
MCRAT2	2	16	11.59	2.75
MCRAT3	6	16	12.63	2.44
MCRAT4	4	16	12.45	2.19
MCRAT5	6	16	11.77	2.21
MCRAT6	3	14	9.05	2.31
CMPANX	0	26	8.69	7.86
SOCIMP	10	32	22.27	4.68
MTHANX	0	38	13.24	9.56
LOCCTL	12	44	22.14	4.27
COGSTL	3	17	12.43	2.86
TRTANX	0	37	15.95	6.83
CMPKNW	0	10	5.09	2.36
CMPEXP	0	18	7.19	4.08
YRSEXP	2	40	17.42	8.72
AGE	24	60	38.38	8.39

Note: MCRATT is simply the sum of MCRAT1 through MCRAT6.

representing high levels of computer anxiety. The range of possible scores on the instrument is 0 (low anxiety) to 40 (high anxiety). For lack of a better measure, one might choose to interpret any scores above the midpoint of 20 as representative of high computer anxiety. There is some basis for selecting this apparently arbitrary value of 20 as a breakpoint between low scores and high scores. Raub (1981) administered the same computer anxiety instrument as was used here to 50 college students prior to their taking a course in COBOL programming. The result was a mean computer usage anxiety score of 20.62. While not wishing to imply that a score from 50 college students can be used as a norm for the general population of managers it is, however, logical (in the absence of better information) to interpret a computer anxiety score of 20 or above as high. Of the 111 managers in the present study, only 3 had scores above 20. Within the context of this interpretation, then, the incidence of computer anxiety in this sample of managers is only 2.7%. This is somewhat at odds with Weinberg's widely reported finding that roughly 30% of managers show some symptoms of cyberphobia, or computer anxiety (see, for example, Paul, 1982). But it is not clear exactly how Weinberg classifies a person as cyberphobic.

Regardless of the norms, breakpoints, or other logical bench marks one may select, it is clear from the present data that the incidence of really serious levels of computer anxiety in managers is surprisingly low. This finding tentatively suggests that the many reports in the business literature of extreme computer anxiety are overblown. Such stories make good reading, but the findings of this study suggest that these extreme cases may be quite rare.

The collective attitude of the managers in the sample toward the impact of computers on society was favorable. Using a rating scale of 0 (unfavorable attitude) to 32 (favorable attitude), the average score of 22.27 indicates a generally positive outlook. There are no broadly based established norms for this quantity, but Raub (1981) obtained an average of 16.92 on this measure using 50 college students. It is reasonable that business managers, who have had opportunities to witness the usefulness of computers in business applications, would form generally more positive attitudes than college students about the impact of computers on society.

The managers' math anxiety was slightly lower than the accepted norm, the locus of control mean of 22.14 corresponded almost exactly with Valecha and Ostrom's (1974) mean of 22.66 (N = 3,694), and the cognitive style mean of 12.43 indicated that the managers in the sample are generally more analytical than heuristic. The trait anxiety score did not differ significantly from established norms. The fact that all of these measures varied only slightly from established norms argues persuasively for the representativeness of the sample of 111 managers.

Computer knowledge and computer experience were measured using new instruments. The aim was simply to produce a spread of knowledge and experience scores that could be used in the subsequent correlation analysis. This aim seems to have been achieved as indicated by the means and standard deviations of these measures as reported in table 8.

Summarizing, the descriptive statistics from the correlates study indicate favorable attitudes toward microcomputers, with some caution expressed about problems with proliferation of hardware and software, surprisingly low levels of computer anxiety, a positive outlook about the impact of computers on society, low math anxiety, values close to the norms for locus of control and trait anxiety, and a tendency for the group to think more analytically than heuristically.

Post Hoc Reliability Calculations

As noted in chapter 3, the reliabilities of the attitudes toward microcomputers, computer anxiety, societal impact, and computer knowledge instruments are not well established. Data obtained from the 111 managers in the correlates study were analyzed to provide information on the actual reliabilities of these new instruments, as well as to provide a check on the reliabilities of the more established instruments.

The quantity used to check for internal consistency was Cronbach's alpha, which is perhaps the most widely used reliability coefficient (Hull and Nie, 1981). Equation (1) gives the computational formula that was used.

$$\alpha = \frac{N}{N-1} \left[1 - \frac{\sum_{i=1}^{N} \sigma_{x_i}}{\sigma_y^2} \right] \qquad (1)$$

where N   =   number of items
       $\sigma_{x_i}^2$ =   variance of item x_i
       σ_y^2 =   variance of test scores

A high value for alpha suggests that the variance among individuals in response to questions is low compared to the total variance in responses. The coefficients presented in table 9 were calculated using SPSS procedure RELIABILITY after the raw responses to individual questions were reversed, where appropriate, by a FORTRAN program written by the author.

Measured reliabilities for the microcomputer attitudes and computer anxiety instruments are excellent, and these results strengthen the findings of the present study because these are the two key variables. The reliability of the societal impact instrument is not quite as good as the reliability of the previous two instruments, but it is still within a range considered acceptable for behavioral research.

The reliability of the locus of control instrument, while not as high as would be desired, is comparable to that measured by the developers of the instrument. Table 9 shows a clear disparity between the reliability of the cognitive style instrument as measured by Barkin (1974) and that measured in the present study. This is because Barkin dichotomized the data (respondents were either analytical or heuristic types) prior to calculating the reliability, whereas in the present study the reliability was calculated using the raw responses to individual items. The latter method will tend to produce much more conservative (and realistic) estimates of reliability. The Kuder-Richardson 20 reliability coefficient is, in fact, theoretically equivalent to Cronbach's alpha when the data are dichotomized.

Cronbach's alpha for trait anxiety is very close to the established reliability for this instrument. The coefficient for the computer knowledge test improved compared to that obtained from the pilot study sample of undergraduate students, and this lends extra credibility to the results of the subsequent correlation analysis.

All of the reliability coefficients given in table 9 are within the range generally considered acceptable for behavioral research. Lowest values are for the two psychological variables, locus of control and cognitive style. Thus, care must be taken in interpreting the results of the upcoming correlation analysis where these two variables are concerned. These possible attenuation effects will be addressed shortly.

Table 9. Results of Reliability Calculations for the Measurement
Instruments

Variable Symbol	Previously Reported Reliability and Method	Measured Reliability (Cronbach's α, N =111)
MCRATT	None	.90
CMPANX	.87, Split-Half, N = 83 See p. 72.	.85
SOCIMP	.74, Split-Half, N = 83 See p. 72.	.76
MTHANX	.89, Split-Half, N = 367 Fennema and Sherman (1976)	.96
LOCCTL	.62, Cronbach's α, N = 3,694 Velecha and Ostrom (1974)	.68
COGSTL	.85, Kuder-Richardson 20, N = 204 Barkin (1974)	.68
TRTANX	.86, Test-Retest, N = 220 Spielberger (1970)	.89
CMPKNW	.60, Split-Half, N = 81 See p. 72.	.78

Post Hoc Factor Analysis for the Attitudes Toward Microcomputers Instrument

Development of the attitudes toward microcomputers instrument was discussed in chapter 3. The technique was to use EMBA students to create an item pool, use the pool to develop a pilot questionnaire, then administer the questionnaire. Using factor analysis on the results of the pilot questionnaire, six important microcomputer attitude factors were tentatively identified and named. The instrument that was used in the field study consisted of 24 of the items from the original pool, 4 items pertaining to each factor. The purpose of the factor analysis was to lend construct validity to the pilot questionnaire.

A post hoc factor analysis of the responses of the 111 managers participating in the field study is useful to check the construct validity of the attitudes questionnaire.

Principal factoring (with iterations) and the varimax rotation method were used (SPSS procedure FACTOR). In this method the main diagonal elements of the correlation matrix are replaced with initial estimates of communalities. The correlation matrix is then successively reduced and the communalities reestimated iteratively until the difference between two successive communality estimates is negligible. This factor analysis identified six factors that each accounted for more than 5% of the total variance, as shown in table 10. It is traditional in factor analysis, though, to ignore factors with eigenvalues less than 1.0. Accordingly, the post hoc factor analysis suggests that the six factors in the original instrument collapsed into three factors that cumulatively account for 76.3% of the variance in the responses. (In the original factor analysis, the six factors that were used accounted for 71.5% of total variance.)

The varimax rotated factor matrix was examined in an effort to understand these three significant factors. Fourteen of the 24 items loaded greater than $|.4|$ on factor 1. On this factor, the items were 2, 5, 8, 11, 14, and 20; on factor 2 they were 15, 17, 18, 21, 23; on factor 3 they were 4, 16, and 22. (The item numbers refer to appendix D.)

The clear theme of post hoc factor 1 is concern about the time required to use a microcomputer. In fact, the word "time" itself appears in five of the six relevant items. This factor is a combination of the original factor 2 (time to use) and factor 5 (more trouble and expense than they're worth). Post hoc factor 2 seems to address the general theme of the usefulness of microcomputers to practicing managers, and consists of a combination of the original factors 3 (lack of capability) and 5 (more trouble and expense than they're worth). Post hoc factor 3 clearly parallels the original factor 4 (using microcomputer not consistent with normal managerial tasks).

These results speak well for the construct validity of the original questionnaire. The post hoc factors represent a combination of the original factors into a smaller number of broader factors. The only exception is that the original main factor (improved access to information) appears only weakly in the post hoc analysis. It must be noted, though, that the original analysis was based on the responses of a group of EMBA students. These respondents are managers who are knowledgeable about the technical and organizational impacts of microcomputers, while the majority of the 111 respondents in the field study on which the post hoc analysis was based are not computer-trained. The field sample managers are not likely to be as sensitive to problems or as well informed about microcomputer capabilities, such as their ability to improve information access, as are EMBA students. Given the greater credibility of the EMBA group, and the fair degree of consistency between the factor analyses, there is no reason to reject the six-factor structure of the original microcomputer attitudes instrument.

Table 10.   Summarized Post Hoc Factor Analysis Results

Factor	Eigenvalue	Percent of Variance	Cumulative Variance
1	7.67	57.3	57.3
2	1.39	10.3	67.6
3	1.16	8.7	76.3
4	0.99	7.4	83.7
5	0.87	6.5	90.2
6	0.68	5.1	95.3

Choice of the Analysis Technique

The objective of the analysis of the correlates data is to obtain statistics that will validly support tests of hypotheses A through Q (see chapter 3). These hypotheses fall into two broad classifications. Hypotheses in the first classification (A through D, F through M, and O through S) are stated in terms of the significance of correlations expected between pairs of variables. Hypotheses in the second group (E and N) are stated in terms of the significance of differences in a dependent variable between groups. The manner in which these hypotheses are stated suggests that those in the first classification should be tested using correlation analysis and those in the second using analysis of variance.

Given the ordinality assumption discussed earlier, Pearson correlation coefficients cannot be validly computed from the field data. Instead, rank order correlations are calculated and used in the hypothesis testing of the correlates study. Spearman's ρ and Kendall's τ are nonparametric rank order correlations that require nothing more than ordinal data and that make no assumptions about the underlying distributions of the variables (Conover, 1980). Both measures are calculated from the ranks rather than from the ordinal data themselves. In fact, Spearman's ρ is exactly the measure obtained by replacing the observed data with their ranks and then computing the Pearson correlation coefficient.

Nie et al. (1975) note that Spearman's ρ is more meaningful than Kendall's τ when there are not a large number of ties at each rank. Examination of the ranked form of the raw data shows a small incidence of ties since most of the variables in the study have a fairly large number of possible scores (MCRATT, for example, ranges from 0 to 96). Hence, the present study uses Spearman's ρ as the measure of correlation between the variables.

Spearman's ρ can be used in support of hypothesis testing (Conover, 1980) when the hypotheses are that pairs of variables are mutually independent (not correlated), as is the case for all the hypotheses of the first classification in this study. SPSS procedure NONPAR CORR implements this.

Results of Hypothesis Tests Based on Correlation Analysis

Tests of hypotheses A through D, F through M, and O through S are made here based on the significance of Spearman's ρ rank order correlation coefficients calculated for pairs of variables using SPSS procedure NONPAR CORR. The input to this procedure was scores on the individual variables that were calculated from the raw data by a FORTRAN program written by the author. Results are shown in table 11.

Table 11 contains information in excess of that needed to test the hypotheses of the correlates study, and there are some interesting results embedded in these additional correlation coefficients. There is, for example, a very significant inverse relationship between computer experience and total years of work experience ($\rho = -.2931, p < .001$), indicating that managers with less total work experience have significantly more computer experience, as would be expected. But these "excess" results are not central to the study, and thus will not be discussed in the text. They are presented for the interested reader who may wish to apply his or her own interpretation to their meaning.

Central to the study are the correlations that involve the hypotheses themselves. The results of the hypothesis testing based on these correlation coefficients are summarized compactly in table 12.

The null hypothesis of Hypothesis A is rejected, indicating that managers with higher levels of computer anxiety tend to have less favorable attitudes toward the usefulness of microcomputers in management. Similarly, it is seen from the rejection of the null hypothesis of Hypothesis B that managers with favorable attitudes toward microcomputers tend also to have favorable attitudes about the impact of computers on society. For hypotheses C, D, F, and G, no significant correlation was found between microcomputer attitudes and math anxiety, age, computer knowledge, or computer experience. It was found, with regard to Hypothesis H, that managers with higher levels of trait anxiety have significantly less favorable attitudes toward microcomputers. The results of the Hypothesis I test show that external locus of control managers have less favorable attitudes toward microcomputers, as suggested in the alternate hypothesis. The null hypothesis of Hypothesis J was not rejected, indicating no relationship between microcomputer attitudes and cognitive style.

Turning to the possible correlates of computer anxiety, it was found in

Table 11. Spearman's ρ Correlation Coefficients from the Field Data (N = 111)

	MCRATT	CMPANX	SOCIMP	MTHANX	LOCCTL	COGSTL	TRTANX	CMPKNW	CMPEXP	YRSEXP	AGE
MCRATT	1.0										
CMPANX	-.2616* (p=.003)	1.0									
SOCIMP	.2486* (p=.004)	-.3781* (p=.001)	1.0								
MTHANX	-.0431 (p=.326)	.3796* (p=.001)	-.1097 (p=.126)	1.0							
LOCCTL	-.1985* (p=.018)	-.0274 (p=.388)	-.0326 (p=.367)	.0233 (p=.404)	1.0						
COGSTL	.0739 (p=.220)	.1037 (p=.139)	-.0111 (p=.454)	.0190 (p=.421)	-.0322 (p=.369)	1.0					
TRTANX	-.1659* (p=.041)	.1135 (p=.118)	-.2182* (p=.011)	.1898* (p=.023)	.2405* (p=.006)	-.0535 (p=.289)	1.0				
CMPKNW	.1034 (p=.140)	-.3780* (p=.001)	.2228* (p=.009)	-.2249* (p=.009)	.1471 (p=.062)	.0396 (p=.340)	-.0896 (p=.175)	1.0			
CMPEXP	.0409 (p=.335)	-.4821* (p=.001)	.1025 (p=.142)	-.2401* (p=.006)	.1116 (p=.112)	-.0317 (p=.371)	-.0590 (p=.269)	.5092* (p=.001)	1.0		
YRSEXP	-.0675 (p=.241)	.1458 (p=.063)	-.1632* (p=.044)	.2299* (p=.008)	-.1549 (p=.052)	.0482 (p=.308)	.0330 (p=.336)	-.2931* (p=.001)	-.2182 (p=.011)	1.0	
AGE	-.0095 (p=.461)	.1848* (p=.026)	-.1362 (p=.077)	.2060* (p=.015)	-.1830* (p=.027)	.0996 (p=.149)	-.0041 (p=.483)	-.2735* (p=.002)	-.2392* (p=.006)	.9175* (p=.001)	1.0

Note: An * indicates correlations that are significant at the 5% level or better.

Table 12.   Results of Hypothesis Tests Based on Correlation Analysis

Hypothesis		Significance	Null Hypothesis
A	-.2616	.003	Rejected
B	.2486*	.004	Rejected
C	-.0431	N.S.	Not Rejected
D	-.0095	N.S.	Not Rejected
F	.1034	N.S.	Not Rejected
G	.0409	N.S.	Not Rejected
H	-.1659*	.041	Rejected
I	-.1985	.018	Rejected
J	.0739	N.S.	Not Rejected
K	-.3781	.001	Rejected
L	.3796	.001	Rejected
M	.1848*	.026	Rejected
O	-.3780*	.001	Rejected
P	-.4821	.001	Rejected
Q	.1135	N.S.	Not Rejected
R	-.0274	N.S.	Not Rejected
S	.0137	N.S.	Not Rejected

*The correlation is probably spurious.

connection with Hypothesis K that there is a strong inverse correlation between computer anxiety and managers' attitudes about the impact of computers on society. Those with higher levels of computer anxiety tended to have a more adverse view of the impact of computers on society. Also very significant was the relationship in Hypothesis L between computer anxiety and math anxiety. High levels of computer anxiety were found to be associated with high levels of math anxiety. The null hypothesis of Hypothesis M was rejected as well, the correlation coefficient indicating that older managers tend to exhibit higher levels of computer anxiety. The null hypothesis of Hypothesis O was ejected. High computer knowledge was found to be associated with low computer anxiety. The null statement of Hypothesis P was strongly rejected, the result indicating that high levels of computer anxiety accompany low levels of computer experience. The null forms of hypotheses Q, R, and S were not rejected, indicating no significant correlations between computer anxiety and trait anxiety, locus of control, or cognitive style.

Summarizing the results thus far, the significant correlates of microcomputer attitudes were found to be computer anxiety (inverse), societal impact attitude (direct), locus of control (internals more favorable), and trait anxiety (inverse). The significant correlates of computer anxiety are societal impact attitude (inverse), math anxiety (direct), computer knowledge (inverse), computer experience (inverse), and age (direct).

Results of Hypothesis Tests Based on Analysis of Variance

Hypotheses E and N are concerned with whether there is any significant difference in microcomputer attitudes or computer anxiety, respectively, between men managers and women managers. These hypotheses were tested using analysis of covariance techniques, with results as reported in tables 13 and 14. The results show clearly that there is no significant difference in microcomputer attitudes for male and female managers, thus the null hypothesis of Hypothesis E is not rejected. The results also show that there is no sex effect with computer anxiety dependent, hence the null hypothesis of Hypothesis N is not rejected. Note that in both of these analyses there are two missing degrees of freedom. This is because two of the survey respondents did not indicate their sex on the questionnaires.

The results of the correlates study are summarized in figure 6, which parallels figure 1, in which the correlates question was originally presented. The arrows appear only where significant correlations were found, and the direction of that correlation is given by the plus or minus sign.

Threats to Validity

Linn and Slinde (1977) identify spurious correlations and attenuation as potential threats to the validity of correlation studies.

Spurious correlations. A spurious correlation occurs when the apparent correlation of variable A with variable B is solely the result of the fact that A also varies with C, and C is indeed the true predictor of B. If the effects of C are somehow controlled for, or held constant, then the correlation between A and B will decrease greatly.

There is a serious threat in the present study that some of the Spearman's ρ correlations may be spurious because of the large number of variables involved, some of which are expected to be inherently interrelated. To check for these spurious correlations, partial correlations were computed for all variable pairs while controlling for all other variables. The resulting partials were then compared with the Spearman zero order correlations. In any cases where the partials differed markedly from the zero order correlations, the zero order correlations were considered as potentially spurious, as will be shown shortly.

There is no SPSS procedure for computing rank partial correlation coefficients, but as Conover (1980) points out, existing computer programs for finding Pearson's partial correlation coefficients may be used on the ranks instead of on the absolute data values. The result is valid Spearman rank partial correlation coefficients. A FORTRAN program written by the author was used to convert the data from the field study into ranks. This data file was

Table 13.   Results of Analysis of Covariance with Microcomputer
Attitude Dependent

Source of Variation	Sum of Squares	DF	Mean Square	F	Significance of F
COVARIATES AGE	41.595	1	41.595	.369	.545
MAIN EFFECTS SEX	168.912	1	168.921	1.497	.224
EXPLAINED	210.507	2	105.254	.933	.397
RESIDUAL	11961.346	106	112.843		
TOTAL	12171.853	108	112.702		

Table 14.   Results of Analysis of Covariance with Computer
Anxiety Dependent

Source of Variation	Sum of Squares	DF	Mean Square	F	Significance of F
COVARIATES AGE	101.599	1	101.599	3.241	.075
MAIN EFFECTS SEX	18.028	1	18.028	.575	.450
EXPLAINED	119.627	2	59.814	1.908	.153
RESIDUAL	3322.978	106	31.349		
TOTAL	3442.605	108	31.876		

then processed using SPSS procedure PARTIAL CORR to produce the partial correlation coefficients.

Unfortunately, the distribution of partial correlation coefficients depends on the underlying multivariate distribution of all the variables used in calculating the partial. This distribution is usually not known, and it is unreasonable to assume that it is multivariate normal in the case of rank partials. Thus, rank partial correlation coefficients cannot be used as test statistics in hypothesis testing (Conover, 1980). Therefore, the hypotheses in this study were tested on the basis of the significance of the Spearman's ρ correlations, but the conclusions thus derived were carefully conditioned in cases where the corresponding partials suggest that spurious correlations might be at play. Table 15 gives the Spearman's ρ zero order correlation coefficients and the accompanying rank order partial correlation coefficients for those correlations that were used in support of hypothesis tests.

Figure 6. Significant Correlates and Their Signs Resulting from the
Field Data Analysis (N = 111) (Not Corrected for
Spurious Correlations)

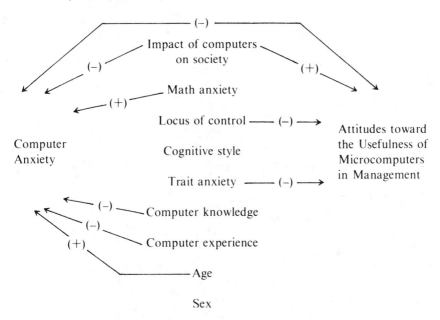

Scanning table 15, it is clear that most of the pairs of zero order and partial correlations are in close agreement, indicating an absence of spurious correlations in these cases. There is no definitive way to determine at what point close agreement ends, but there are four variable pairs for which there is enough disagreement that spuriousness could cause erroneous hypothesis tests: MCRATT-SOCIMP, MCRATT-TRTANX, CMPANX-CMPKNW, and CMPANX-AGE.

For the MCRATT-SOCIMP pair, the most plausible source of spuriousness is as shown in figure 7. These correlations indicate that high MCRATT scores will be associated with low CMPANX scores, which are in turn accompanied by high SOCIMP scores. This phenomenon could give an inflated impression of the covariance between MCRATT and SOCIMP. The spuriousness would be indicated by the dashed line. With the spuriousness controlled for, the partial is only .1257. The existence of the spuriousness mechanism as it is shown in figure 8 was confirmed by recomputing the MCRATT-SOCIMP partial correlation coefficient, controlling for all other variables *except* CMPANX. In this case the MCRATT-SOCIMP correlation increased to .2093, confirming that the CMPANX variable is the source of the spuriousness. While, as was said earlier, it is not strictly valid to base

Table 15. Comparisons of Zero Order and Partial Rank Correlation
Coefficients for Correlates Study Hypotheses

Variable Pair	Zero Order Spearman's (Significance) (N = 111)	Partial (DF = 101)
MCRATT-CMPANX	-.2616 (p=.003)	-.2191
MCRATT-SOCIMP	.2486 (p=.004)	.1257
MCRATT-MTHANX	-.0431 (p=.326)	.0701
MCRATT-LOCCTL	-.1985 (p=.018)	-.1792
MCRATT-COGSTL	.0739 (p=.220)	.0937
MCRATT-TRTANX	-.1659 (p=.041)	-.0747
MCRATT-CMPKNW	.1034 (p=.140)	.0450
MCRATT-CMPEXP	.0409 (p=.335)	-.0808
MCRATT-AGE	-.0095 (p=.461)	-.0070
CMPANX-SOCIMP	-.3781 (p=.001)	-.3120
CMPANX-MTHANX	.3796 (p=.001)	.3013
CMPANX-LOCCTL	-.0274 (p=.338)	.0000
CMPANX-COGSTL	.1037 (p=.139)	.1321
CMPANX-TRTANX	.1135 (p=.118)	-.0529
CMPANX-CMPKNW	-.3780 (p=.001)	-.0855
CMPANX-CMPEXP	-.4821 (p=.001)	-.3697
CMPANX-AGE	.1848 (p=.026)	-.0265

Figure 7. Possible Source of Spuriousness in the MCRATT-
SOCIMP Zero Order Correlation

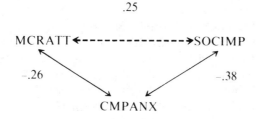

Figure 8. Possible Sources of Spuriousness in the MCRATT-
TRTANX Zero Order Correlation

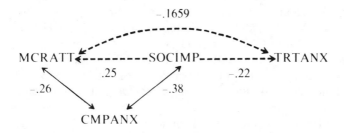

hypothesis tests on the partials, it is clear that if the partial *were* a zero order correlation, its significance would only be approximately .13. Thus there is sufficient evidence that the MCRATT-SOCIMP correlation is spurious to reverse the hypothesis test and conclude that the null hypothesis of Hypothesis B should *not* be rejected.

The MCRATT-TRTANX pair may also be spurious, as shown in figure 8. Here, the probable mechanism is that high MCRATT scores are associated with high SOCIMP scores (explainable either through the spurious or the legitimate correlations shown in the diagram), which are in turn associated with low TRTANX scores. This could give the false appearance of a larger than actual inverse relationship between MCRATT and TRTANX. The zero order MCRATT-TRTANX correlation is barely significant (.041); thus, the removal of any spuriousness in this variable pair would reverse the hypothesis test (Hypothesis H). Removing CMPANX as a controlling variable resulted in a MCRATT-TRTANX partial correlation of –.10. This shows that the figure 8 mechanism only partly explains the spuriousness mechanism. Nonetheless, there is sufficient evidence to reverse the test of Hypothesis H, and it is concluded that there is no significant relationship between MCRATT and TRTANX.

There is a glaring difference between the zero order and partial correlations for the CMPANX-CMPKNW variable pair. As figure 9 shows, there are several plausible paths of spurious influence. The spuriousness mechanism diagrammed in figure 9 was tested by recomputing the CMPANX-CMPKNW partial correlation three times, successively removing CMPEXP, MTHANX, and SOCIMP from the list of controlling variables. With CMPEXP removed, the partial correlation changed from –.0855 to –.2650, confirming that CMPEXP is primarily responsible for causing the spuriousness. Removing MTHANX from the controlling variables list yielded a partial correlation of –.3005, and removing SOCIMP gave a result of –.3321. These tests establish that the mechanism shown in figure 9 is correct and provide a firm basis for reversing the test of Hypothesis O. There is no legitimate correlation between CMPANX and CMPKNW.

Finally, it appears from the table 15 data that the CMPANX-AGE zero order correlation may be spurious, with the possible mechanism as given in figure 10. In this case, the possible mechanism could not be successfully verified. With both CMPEXP and MTHANX removed as controlling variables, the CMPANX-AGE partial correlation was still only .0594, indicating that the source of the spuriousness was more complex than suggested in figure 10. Even without discovering the exact cause of the spuriousness, however, there is such a striking difference between the partial and zero order correlation for this variable pair that the hypothesis test must be reversed and the null hypothesis of Hypothesis M not be rejected.

Studies that depend upon correlation analysis seldom recognize the threat to validity posed by spurious correlations. Their impact is clear here in that, through an examination of the results for spurious correlations, four erroneous conclusions have been avoided. Figure 11 shows the final results of the correlates study, corrected for spuriousness.

Attenuation. Attenuation, the second threat to the validity of correlation analyses, is depression in the value of correlations that is caused by unreliable measurement of variables (Lord, 1963). This has the effect of causing type II errors in hypothesis testing.

In the present study, attenuation would threaten the results of the hypothesis tests only in cases where the significance of the Spearman's ρ was borderline on the high side and when one of the two variables was measured using an instrument of questionable reliability. No such cases occurred here, as is seen by examining the correlation coefficients in table 15, conditioned for spurious effects. Hence attenuation does not appear to be at play in the specific hypothesis testing situations in the study.

Figure 9.   Possible Sources of Spuriousness in the CMPANX-
CMPKNW Zero Order Correlation

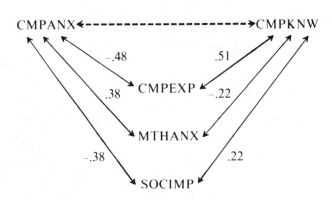

Figure 10.   Possible Sources of Spuriousness in the CMPANX-
AGE Zero Order Correlation

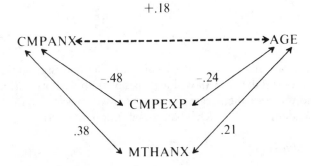

Pre-Post Study

This section describes the analysis techniques and results for the pre-post
laboratory study. A short summary of these results appears at the end of the
chapter.

Variables

Table 16 lists the variables involved specifically in the pre-post component of
the study. These variables are derived from the list of variables given in table 7.
As explained earlier, this analysis will take the conservative view that all of

Figure 11. Significant Correlates and Their Signs Resulting from
the Field Data Analysis (N = 111) (Corrected for
Spurious Correlations)

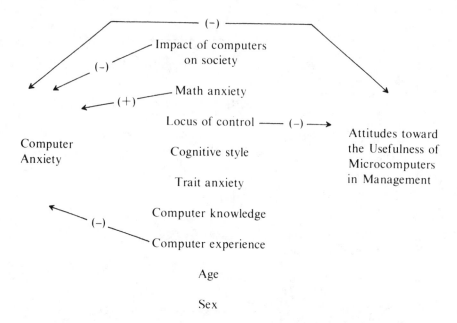

these variables can, at best, be treated as ordinal. The analysis techniques to be used on the pre-post data are all various types of analysis of variance, which is generally more robust then regression analysis with respect to the use of an ordinal dependent variable (Kleinbaum and Kupper, 1978).

Descriptive Statistics

Table 17 summarizes the overall descriptive statistics for the pre-post data. These data are presented separately for the two participating EMBA classes, the members of which are further subdivided by the four psychological types. The dichotomizations of internal and external locus of control and heuristic and analytical cognitive style were done at the median scores for the 67 participating EMBA students. Scores for the treatment and control groups are shown separately. A cursory examination of these data suggests that the treatment did not seem significantly to improve microcomputer attitudes or reduce computer anxiety. Firm conclusions on these questions must, however, await more sophisticated analysis.

The EMBA classes consisted of a mix of managers and nonmanagers, as

Table 16.   Variables Used in Pre-Post Component of the Study

PREANX	Pretest computer anxiety
PSTANX	Posttest computer anxiety
PREATT	Pretest attitude toward microcomputers
PSTATT	Posttest attitude toward microcomputers
LOCCTL	Locus of control score
COGSTL	Cognitive style score

determined by the job titles that the student respondents entered on the pretest questionnaire. A respondent with a job title of "stress engineer" definitely did not fall into the managerial classification, while one giving a title of "manager—quality control" clearly did. Borderline cases were assumed to be nonmanagers. This classification method yielded 39 managers and 28 nonmanagers. Table 18 presents the pre-post descriptive statistics with the four psychological types aggregated but separated by job type (manager versus nonmanager). These data suggest that there may be important differences between the managers and the nonmanagers, in that the managers appear to have generally lower microcomputer attitude scores and higher levels of computer anxiety than the nonmanagers. This makes sense in the context of this experiment because nearly all of the nonmanagers have engineering backgrounds and are thus understandably comfortable with computers. These differences are even more vivid when the two EMBA classes are combined to produce the summarized descriptive statistics shown in table 19. (The statistical justification for combining the two classes will be given shortly.)

It is clear from table 19 that the managers have substantially higher levels of computer anxiety than the nonmanagers. If this can be statistically verified, then it becomes reasonable to analyze the experimental results separately for the two groups. Prior to doing this, however, an analysis technique must be selected and justified.

Choice of the Analysis Technique

The objective of the analysis of the data from the pre-post study is to apply statistical techniques so as to permit valid tests of the following hypotheses, restated here for convenience.

Table 17. Descriptive Statistics from the Pre-Post Study

Attitude Toward Microcomputers

		Internal/Heuristic (N=17)			Internal/Analytical (N=18)			External/Heuristic (N=14)			External/Analytical (N=18)		
		Pretest Mean	Posttest Mean	Change in Means	Pretest Mean	Posttest Mean	Change in Means	Pretest Mean	Posttest Mean	Change in Means	Pretest Mean	Posttest Mean	Change in Means
EMBA Class I	T	(6) 71.5	69.3	-2.2	(6) 79.2	81.5	+2.3	(4) 71.5	71.8	+0.3	(3) 76.0	78.0	+2.0
	C	(5) 76.8	78.0	+1.2	(2) 72.5	73.0	+0.5	(6) 70.2	68.7	-1.5	(3) 82.3	79.3	-3.0
EMBA Class II	T	(2) 54.5	60.5	+6.0	(5) 77.8	78.8	+1.0	(4) 70.5	68.3	-2.2	(5) 73.2	69.2	-4.0
	C	(4) 71.3	67.8	-3.5	(5) 77.2	76.2	-1.0	(0) -	-	-	(7) 75.7	73.3	-2.4

Computer Anxiety

		Internal/Heuristic (N=17)			Internal/Analytical (N=18)			External/Heuristic (N=14)			External/Analytical (N=18)		
		Pretest Mean	Posttest Mean	Change in Means	Pretest Mean	Posttest Mean	Change in Means	Pretest Mean	Posttest Mean	Change in Means	Pretest Mean	Posttest Mean	Change in Means
EMBA Class I	T	(6) 9.7	9.2	-0.5	(6) 6.8	6.0	-0.8	(4) 10.0	7.5	-2.5	(3) 7.0	5.7	-1.3
	C	(5) 4.0	5.4	+1.4	(2) 10.0	9.5	-0.5	(6) 8.5	9.7	+1.2	(3) 5.7	6.3	+0.6
EMBA Class II	T	(2) 5.0	5.5	+0.5	(5) 3.0	3.6	+0.6	(4) 13.3	13.8	+0.5	(5) 9.6	10.4	+0.8
	C	(4) 8.3	8.5	+0.2	(5) 9.8	9.2	-0.6	(0) -	-	-	(7) 7.7	9.7	+2.0

Note: "T" denotes treatment group. "C" control group. The number in each subgroup follows in parentheses.

Table 18. Descriptive Statistics from the Pre-Post Study
(Managers versus Nonmanagers)

		Pretest Attitude Mean	Posttest Attitude Mean	Change in Means	Pretest Anxiety Mean	Posttest Anxiety Mean	Change in Means
EMBA Class I							
Managers	C(8)	71.5	70.1	-1.4	10.1	13.0	2.9
	T(11)	71.2	71.4	0.2	11.5	10.1	-1.4
Nonmanagers	C(8)	78.3	78.1	-0.2	3.4	2.4	-1.0
	T(8)	79.4	80.1	0.7	4.1	3.4	-0.7
EMBA Class II							
Managers	C(10)	74.4	71.2	-3.2	9.2	10.4	1.2
	T(10)	69.0	67.0	-2.0	9.2	10.2	1.0
Nonmanagers	C(6)	76.2	75.5	-0.7	7.3	7.8	0.5
	T(6)	76.0	77.5	1.5	5.7	5.7	0.0

Note: "T" denotes treatment group, "C" control group.

Table 19. Summary Descriptive Statistics from the Pre-Post Study

		Pretest Attitude Mean	Posttest Attitude Mean	Change in Means	Pretest Anxiety Mean	Posttest Anxiety Mean	Change in Means
Managers	C(18)	73.1	70.7	-2.4	9.6	11.6	2.0
	T(21)	70.1	69.3	-0.8	10.4	10.1	-0.3
Nonmanagers	C(14)	77.4	77.0	-0.4	5.1	4.7	-0.4
	T(14)	77.9	79.0	1.1	4.8	4.4	-0.4

Note: "T" denotes treatment group, "C" control group.

Hypothesis T (P-P,3)

H_o: There will be no significant change in managers' attitudes toward their using microcomputers in management as a result of a brief training session on microcomputers and microcomputer-based management software.

H_a: The managers will have a significantly more favorable attitude toward using microcomputers after the training session.

There are two additional subhypotheses related to Hypotheses T that will be tested if the null hypothesis of T is rejected.

Hypothesis T′ (P-P,3)

H_o: There will be no significant difference between the attitude change of internal locus of control managers versus external locus of control managers.

H_a: Internal locus of control managers will experience significantly more improvement in attitude than external locus of control managers.

Hypothesis T″ (P-P,3)

H_o: There will no significant difference between the attitude change of analytical cognitive style managers versus heuristic cognitive style managers.

H_a: Analytical cognitive style managers will experience significantly more improvement in attitude than heuristic cognitive style managers.

Hypothesis U (P-P,5)

This hypothesis is identicial to Hypothesis T except that the phrase "managers" attitudes toward their using microcomputers in management" in the null hypothesis should be replaced by "managers' level of computer anxiety." The microcomputer attitude variable in the alternate hypothesis should be replaced by the level of computer anxiety variable.

Hypothesis V (P-P,4)

H_o: There is no significant difference in the treatment group between managers with high and low computer anxiety in the amount of attitude change that results from the training course on microcomputers.

H_a: High computer anxiety managers experience significantly less attitude improvement from the training course than do managers with low pretreatment anxiety.

As discussed in chapter 3, the design of the laboratory study is a classic pretest-posttest control group design with two factors, each having two levels, with random assignment of subjects to the treatment and control groups. The two factors are EMBA class (I or II) and group (control or treatment). Analysis of pre-post laboratory data can be approached in one of three ways: repeated measures analysis of variance, analysis of variance on the difference scores, and analysis of covariance.

The first method is a traditional ANOVA with the pretest and posttest measurements representing the repeated measures factor. This is historically the standard technique for analysis of pre-post data, but this method has been seriously discredited (Huck and McLean, 1975). Huck and McLean's criticisms of the repeated measures technique are twofold. First, since pretest scores are collected before the treatment is administered, there is no way for any treatment or interaction effects to affect the pretest scores. Yet, there are terms for these two effects in the repeated measures model. Second, since the posttest scores may not be thought of as having an interaction component because the treatment effects influence only the posttest data, the F test for the main effect of treatments will be substantially too conservative. This is because the similarity between the pretest means (as a result of random assignment of subjects to groups) will cause the differences between the posttest means to become distributed over the two trials. As Huck and McLean emphasize, this means that the estimated treatment effects will be only about half as large as they should be. Because of the conservative F in the test for treatment effects, the probability of a type II error (accepting the null when the alternate is true) will be inflated. The authors cite studies in which these misleading statistical effects of repeated measures analysis of variance have caused researchers to make erroneous conclusions in hypothesis tests. Huck and McLean thus completely condemn use of this technique for analysis of pre-post laboratory data, stating that the main effect of trial F that comes from a repeated measures ANOVA is results that are "worthless" from an experimental point of view.

In an effort to avoid the above problems, some researchers have abandoned repeated measures ANOVA in favor of a traditional ANOVA on the difference scores. Difference or "gain" scores are derived by subtracting the pretest score from the posttest score for each individual subject. Huck and McLean note that an ANOVA on gain scores, while not yielding any information beyond that obtained from repeated measures, is straightforward and noncontroversial compared with repeated measures ANOVA. Linn and Slinde (1977) have, however, identified two shortcomings of the difference score approach.

First, difference scores are usually negatively correlated with the pretest scores. This is because large positive differences are more likely to be observed for persons with low initial scores, while those with high initial scores are less likely to exhibit these large positive differences. As Bereiter (1963) points out, this means that a grouping of subjects with high difference scores would contain an overrepresentation of people with low pretest scores.

Second, Linn and Slinde have shown that the reliability of difference scores is seriously depressed when the pretest and posttest scores are correlated. Specifically, ρ_{DD}' is given by

$$\rho_{DD'} = \frac{\rho - \rho_{xy}}{1 - \rho_{xy}} \qquad (2)$$

where $\rho_{DD'}$ = reliability of difference scores
         ρ_{xy} = prescore postscore correlation
assuming $\sigma_x = \sigma_y$ and $\sigma_{xx'} = \sigma_{yy'} = \rho$

It is clear from equation (2) that $\rho_{DD'}$ drops as ρ_{xy} increases. A low ρ_{xy}, however, raises the question of whether the pre and post measures are really getting at the same construct. Because of this artifact, where a pre-post study with high construct validity yields difference scores of inherently low reliability, it is not desirable to perform tests of important hypotheses based on an analysis of difference scores. In fact, Linn and Slinde comment that when treatment groups are formed by random assignment, the posttest *alone* is "perfectly suitable" as a dependent variable, and that if pretest measures are available, their potential usefulness is merely to increase the power of the statistical test.

Huck and McLean (1975) argue convincingly that the third approach, analysis of covariance, is the preferred method for analyzing pre-post laboratory study data. In this approach, the pretest scores are included as a covariate. This test provides the same information as the gain score analysis, but is statistically more powerful and thus more sensitive to the effect of the experimental treatment. ANOVA on gain scores is a weaker test, and repeated measures is an incorrect test.

Thus the present analysis will be performed using ANCOVA (analysis of covariance) techniques. The pretest scores are the covariate, and they are used to adjust the posttest means to account for any initial differences between the control and treatment groups and to increase the power of the F tests by decreasing within-group variability.

Analysis of covariance suffers from a set of relatively restrictive assumptions, as Elashoff (1969) aptly explains. Violations of these assumptions represent potential threats to the validity of the conclusions that will be made based on the ANCOVA on the pre-post data. Accordingly, these assumptions must be carefully checked, as will be discussed shortly.

The choice of ANCOVA as an analysis technique in the present study is further reinforced by the findings of Feldt (1958). Feldt compared blocking, ANOVA on difference scores, and ANCOVA, and found the ANCOVA approach to have the greatest precision when the correlation between the pretest and posttest scores is greater than about 0.6. For the laboratory data the pre-post correlation was .85 for microcomputer attitudes and .84 for computer anxiety (N = 67), confirming the appropriateness of the ANCOVA approach.

Results of Hypothesis Tests Based on Analysis of Covariance

As is clearly stated in all the hypotheses, the study is restricted solely to managers. Yet the laboratory sample consisted of managers and nonmanagers, and the descriptive statistics in table 19 suggest that there may be important differences in computer attitudes and anxiety between these two groups. This difference was verified to be statistically significant by running two simple analyses of variance with microcomputer attitude and computer anxiety, respectively, as the dependent variable and job group (manager versus nonmanager) independent. The main effect of job group was significant at the $p < .008$ and $p < .000$ levels, respectively. This indicates that the characteristics of the nonmanagers are so different that they should be excluded from subsequent analysis of the laboratory study results. Thus, to keep the study strictly in accordance with the stated hypotheses (managers only), the 28 nonmanagers were dropped from the analysis, leaving a sample of 39 managers.

These 39 managers belonged to two separate EMBA classes. Two further analyses of variance were performed to determine whether the participants in the two classes were sufficiently similar to justify pooling the classes. With posttest attitude (PSTATT) dependent and PREATT as a covariate, the main effect for classes was not significant ($F = 2.01$, $p < .162$). For computer anxiety dependent, the class effect was even less significant ($F = .03$, $p < .861$). Based on this justification, the 39 managers from the two EMBA classes were pooled into a single group for hypothesis testing.

The null form of Hypothesis T (no change in microcomputer attitudes) was tested using an analysis of covariance with PSTATT dependent, PREATT, LOCCTL, and COGSTL as covariates, and GROUP (control versus treatment) as the main effect. Table 20 presents the results of this ANCOVA. Obviously, the main effect was not significant, so the null form of Hypotheses T is not rejected, supporting the conclusion that there was no significant difference in change in attitude toward microcomputers between the control and treatment groups. Since the null hypothesis is not rejected, there is no reason to test the subhypotheses T' and T''. This result is consistent with the findings of many behaviorists and psychologists that attitude change, if it can be achieved at all, requires an extended period of time, as will be discussed in chapter 5.

The null statement of Hypothesis U (no change in computer anxiety) was tested similarly with results as shown in table 21. In this case the main effect is significant ($p < .028$), indicating that the null statement of Hypothesis U should be rejected. Here there *is* a significant difference in the change in computer anxiety between the control and treatment groups. This result must be interpreted very carefully, however, because the ANCOVA indicates only

Table 20.   ANCOVA Output for Test of Hypothesis T

Source of Variation	Sum of Squares	DF	Mean Square	F	Signif. of F
Covariates	2081.457	3	693.819	22.524	0.000
PREATT	1651.068	1	1651.068	53.599	0.000
LOCCTL	0.426	1	0.426	0.014	0.907
COGSTL	22.552	1	22.552	0.732	0.398
Main Effects	9.976	1	9.976	0.324	0.573
GROUP	9.976	1	9.976	0.325	0.573
Explained	2091.433	4	522.858	16.974	0.000
Residual	1047.377	34	30.804		
Total	3138.770	38	82.599		

Table 21.   ANCOVA Output for Test of Hypothesis U

Source of Variation	Sum of Squares	DF	Mean Square	F	Signif. of F
Covariates	487.995	3	162.665	17.730	0.000
PREANX	378.369	1	378.369	41.240	0.000
LOCCTL	25.051	1	25.051	2.730	0.108
COGSTL	0.001	1	0.001	0.000	0.990
Main Effects	48.424	1	48.424	5.278	0.028
GROUP	48.424	1	48.424	5.278	0.028
Explained	536.419	4	134.105	14.617	0.000
Residual	311.940	34	9.175		
Total	848.359	38	22.325		

the presence of a significant difference, and says nothing about the direction of that difference or whether the change was in the control group, in the treatment group, or both.

The pre-post control group design employed here seeks to provide a stable reference (the control group) against which changes in the treatment group may be contrasted. The aim is that the control group members will be immune to any training they may receive between the pretest and the posttest. This was not the case in the present study.

As was explained in chapter 3, the control group was given an introductory lecture in BASIC programming while the other half of each EMBA class received the experimental treatment, which consisted of the microcomputer demonstration and the hands-on training. As the descriptive statistics of table 19 reveal, the BASIC lecture actually had a bigger impact on the control group's computer anxiety than the demonstration and hands-on experience had on the treatment group. In fact, the BASIC lecture substantially increased the computer anxiety level, while the treatment only marginally reduced it. This difference between the groups is the significant effect that the ANCOVA uncovered, but the change was not in the expected group and was not in the expected direction.

Ideally, the control group should have been given a lecture on a topic completely neutral to computers and information systems, but the experimental conditions did not permit this to be done. The EMBA program operates on a highly compressed time schedule and it was not possible to sacrifice half of an entire class meeting to a non-computer-related topic in support of an experiment. It would be valuable to replicate this experiment at some future time in an experimental setting that would permit completely neutral handling of the control group.

This unexpected change in the computer anxiety level of the control group versus the treatment group requires that the null form of Hypothesis U, as it is strictly stated, not be rejected. This null hypothesis was that there would be significant change in the managers' computer anxiety level as a result of the training session on microcomputers. There was, in fact, no such change in the treatment group—the change occurred in the control group, and that was the effect that was picked up by the ANCOVA results of table 21.

The unexpected result in this part of the experiment is, however, of value along several dimensions. First, it can be concluded that a brief training session is of minimal value in treating computer anxiety. This result is consistent with Weinberg (1981), who holds that successful treatment of computer anxiety in managers requires a period of months. Second, it is clear from the experiment that training in a programming language such as BASIC is *not* the place to start indoctrination of newcomers to computing, because this increases computer anxiety and the accompanying barriers to learning. Third, the results revealed that the managers in the sample reacted differently to both activities in the control group and in the treatment group in contrast to the nonmanagers. In fact, there was no significant microcomputer attitude or computer anxiety effect whatsoever when the preceeding ANCOVAs were run for the nonmanagers. This underscores the need to approach very carefully the indoctrination of managers to computing. Further implications of all these results will be discussed in the next chapter.

Hypothesis V addressed the question of whether the treatment would have different effects on the high anxiety managers versus the low anxiety managers. The division between the high and low computer anxiety groups was done at the median score of 7.4. This was the only rational approach for dichotomizing the scores because there are no established norms for this computer anxiety instrument as applied to managers, other than those resulting from this study. Results of the ANCOVA appear in table 22.

The implicit assumption of no significant difference in computer anxiety change between the two intact EMBA classes was tested again here, and that difference was again found to be not significant ($F = 0.71, p < .41$). The results show that the null hypothesis of Hypothesis V should not be rejected, as there was no significant difference in computer anxiety change between the high and low anxiety groups. This result is not surprising in light of the earlier finding that the training session had a minimal impact on the managers' level of computer anxiety.

Summarizing the hypothesis testing results, it is seen that none of the three laboratory study hypotheses (T, U, V) was rejected. A significant result was discovered in connection with the Hypothesis U test, but this was found to be spurious because of the change that occurred in the control group.

Threats to Validity

The results of the pre-post component of this study are threatened by errors in the statistical analysis techniques employed and by possible flaws in the design and execution of the experiment.

Statistical threats. Analysis of covariance is a powerful statistical technique, but it is quite sensitive to violations of key assumptions. Elashoff (1969) provides an excellent summary of the "critical" and "necessary" assumptions of analysis of covariance, which are shown in figure 12. Critical assumptions are crucial to the underlying rationale for the use of analysis of covariance; necessary assumptions lend statistical simplicity and assure the validity of standard statistical tests.

Randomization, a critical assumption, assumes random assignment of individuals to treatments. Random assignment balances the effect of all unidentified or unmeasurable variables equally upon the control and treatment groups.

Test: Comparison for equality of means of the control and treatment groups.

Impact: Violation of this assumption can cause linear correlation between treatment effects and covariate means, thus violating the assumption of homogeniety of regression.

Remedy: Covariance adjustment procedures (Evans and Anastasio, 1968).

Table 22.   ANCOVA Output for Test of Hypothesis V

Source of Variation	Sum of Squares	DF	Mean Square	F	Signif. of F
Covariates	1347.857	1	1347.857	29.525	0.000
PREATT	1347.857	1	1347.857	29.525	0.000
Main Effects	37.961	2	28.980	0.416	0.667
CLASS	32.271	1	32.271	0.707	0.413
ANXGRP	0.830	1	0.830	0.018	0.894
2-Way Interactiosn	1.577	1	1.577	0.035	0.855
CLASS ANXGRP	1.577	1	1.577	0.035	0.885
EXPLAINED	1387.395	4	346.849	7.598	0.001
RESIDUAL	730.415	16	45.651		
TOTAL	2117.810	20	105.890		

Figure 12.   Assumptions of Analysis of Covariance

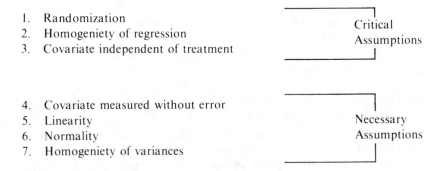

1. Randomization
2. Homogeniety of regression   } Critical Assumptions
3. Covariate independent of treatment

4. Covariate measured without error
5. Linearity   } Necessary Assumptions
6. Normality
7. Homogeniety of variances

Lack of randomization is not considered a threat in the present study because, although the EMBA classes are intact groups, the assignment to the control and treatment groups within classes was done randomly. The experimenter used a table of random numbers from the CRC standard mathematics tables in conjunction with the EMBA class rosters to make assignments to the groups prior to the experiment.

Homogeneity of regression, the second critical assumption, is often called the assumption of equal slopes. The assumption is that there is no significant interaction between treatment group and slope (i.e., the slope of the regression line is equal for all treatment groups).

Test: Compare scatterplots for each treatment group.
Impact: Understatement of the between treatments F.
Remedy: Change the model and run separate regressions of each group (Atiqullah, 1964).

Scatterplots were prepared for each of the treatment groups in each of the two EMBA classes, one set for microcomputer attitudes and one set for computer anxiety. The dependent variable was plotted on the ordinate and the covariate on the abscissa. Inspection of these scatterplots, as recommended by Elashoff, did not reveal evidence of any substantial treatment-slope interaction. If such an interaction were present, it would result in an understatement of the between class effects. Any interaction would have to be extremely strong to affect the study results because the class effect in the present study was extremely weak for both microcomputer attitudes and computer anxiety, as was discussed earlier. Hence, homogeneity of regression is not threatened here.

The third critical assumption, that the covariate is independent of treatment, means that all of the X_i (here, all of the pretest scores) should be statistically independent of the treatment.

Test: Check method of assignment to groups.
Impact: Probable violation of the homogeneity of regression assumption, resulting in understatement of the between treatments F.

This assumption is not violated in the present study because the random assignment to groups method was employed.

The foregoing three critical assumptions of analysis of covariance are clearly upheld in the study. That the covariate is measured without error is the first of the necessary assumptions and means that the model assumes perfect accuracy in the measurement of the covariate. Since the covariate is introduced to try to reduce variability in the estimate of the dependent variable, the implications of incorrect measurement of the covariate are obvious.

Test: Indirectly, the reliability scores for the attitude toward microcomputers and computer anxiety instruments provide measures of the accuracy of measurement of the covariate. There is no way to ascertain the absolute accuracy of a psychometric instrument.
Impact: Understatement of the between treatments F.

Remedy: Lord (1963) says that if the covariate cannot be measured reliably, it should be controlled experimentally by randomization if possible.

In this study the threat of violation of this assumption is minimized by use of random assignment of subjects to control and treatment groups. The reliabilities of the microcomputer attitudes and computer anxiety instruments were .90 and .85, respectively (Cronbach's alpha), as reported earlier, and their construct validity was established to the extent possible using factor analytic techniques. This assumption would have to be violated very seriously before it would cause any change in the conclusions of the study.

Linearity, the second necessary assumption, simply assumes that there is a linear relationship between the covariate and the dependent variable.

Test: Scatterplots.
Impact: Understatement of the between treatments F.
Remedy: Use of quadratic or cubic terms in the regression model.

The scatterplots revealed the linear model to be appropriate. Additionally, the significance of the F for the pretest score as covariate was .000 with both microcomputer attitudes and computer anxiety dependent, indicating that the covariates were successfully explaining large proportions of the total variance under the assumption of the linear model.

The third of the necessary assumptions, normality, assumes that within each group, at each level, the values of the dependent variable are normally distributed.

Test: Skewness and kurtosis (third and fourth moments).
Impact: Minimal. Atiqullah (1964) found that nonnormality in the distribution of Ys has little effect on the F for main effects when the covariate scores are normal.
Remedy: None.

For the pretest microcomputer attitude scores, skewness and kurtosis were 0.026 and 0.288, respectively, indicating essentially no skewness and a curve that is just slightly more peaked than normal. The same measures for the pretest computer anxiety scores were 0.448 and –0.412. Here, the distribution was skewed to the left because lower computer anxiety scores predominated, and was more broad than the standard normal distribution. This represents a not inconsequential departure of the distribution of the pretest computer anxiety scores from normality. There is, however, no easy remedy short of

Figure 13. Summarized Results of the Correlates Study

Characterization of the Sample

N = 111
Average Age: 38.4

Sex: 90 Male, 19 Female, 2 not indicating sex
Average Years of Work Experience: 17.4

Attitude toward Microcomputers

Mean Microcomputer Attitudes Score: 69.0. Minimum possible was 0, maximum 96, indicating managers' generally positive attitudes about the usefulness of microcomputers in management. The least positive response was on the factor that expressed concerns about compatibility problems that could result from uncontrolled proliferation of microcomputer hardware and software.

Incidence of Computer Anxiety

Mean Computer Anxiety Score: 8.7. Minimum possible was 0, maximum 40, indicating managers' generally low level of computer anxiety. Defining "high" computer anxiety as a score above the middle of this range (20), the incidence of computer anxiety in managers was only 2.7%. This indicates that the problem is not nearly as widespread or severe as many articles in the business press suggest.

Other Descriptive Statistics

The other descriptive statistics indicated low collective scores on math anxiety, a positive outlook about the impact of computers on society, nominal values on locus of control, trait anxiety, computer knowledge, and computer experience, and a tendency to think more analytically than heuristically.

Measures Cronbach's α Reliabilities (N = 111)

MCRATT	.90	SOCIMP	.76	LOCCTL	.68	TRTANX	.89
CMPANX	.85	MTHANX	.96	COGSTL	.68	CMPKNW	.78

Figure 13. (continued)

Post Hoc Factor Structure of Microcomputer Attitudes Questionnaire Responses

Factor	Eigenvalue	Cum. Variance	Source
1	7.67	57.3	Combination of original factors 2 and 5.
2	1.39	67.6	Combination of original factors 3 and 5.
3	1.16	76.3	Closely resembles original factor 4.

Significant Correlates of Attitudes toward Microcomputers (Corrected for Spuriousness)

Computer Anxiety
$\rho = -.2616, p = .003$

Locus of Control
$\rho = -.1985, p = .018$

Interpretation: Less favorable microcomputer attitudes are accompanied by higher levels of computer anxiety, and vice versa. Internal locus of control managers have more favorable attitudes toward microcomputers than external locus of control managers.

Significant Correlates of Computer Anxiety (Corrected for Spuriousness)

Attitude toward Microcomputers
$\rho = -.2616, p = .003$

Impact of Computers on Society
$\rho = -.3781, p = .001$

Math Anxiety
$\rho = .3796, p = .001$

Computer Experience
$\rho = -.4821, p = .001$

Interpretation: Managers with higher levels of computer anxiety have less favorable assessments of the probable impact of computers on society. Math anxiety and computer anxiety appear to occur together. Managers with higher levels of computer experience have substantially lower levels of computer anxiety.

Possible Compromising Threats to Validity

None

Figure 14. Summarized Results of the Pre-Post Study

Characterization of the Sample

N = 67   Sex: 58 Male, 9 Female
Average Age: 32.8   Average Years of Work Experience: 11.0
Composition: 39 Managers,
    28 Nonmanagers

Descriptive Statistics
(Managers Only)

	Pretest Attitude Mean	Posttest Attitude Mean	Change in Means	Pretest Anxiety Mean	Posttest Anxiety Mean	Change in Means
Control Group	73.1	70.7	–2.4	9.6	11.6	2.0
Treatment Group	70.1	69.3	–0.8	10.4	10.1	–0.3

Hypothesis Tests

Hypothesis T   (No significant change in microcomputer attitudes): Not
                 Rejected.

Hypothesis U   (No significant change in computer anxiety): Not Rejected.
                 Note: A significant ($p < .028$) computer anxiety effect was
                       discovered by the ANCOVA, but the effect was
                       purious because of the instability in the control group
                       scores.

Hypothesis V   (No difference in treatment effect for high versus low anxiety
                 managers): Not Rejected.

Miscellaneous Findings

The increase in computer anxiety and decrease in favorableness of
microcomputer attitudes in the control group as a result of the lecture on
BASIC clearly indicate that initial training in programming is not the best way
to begin indoctrination of managers to computers.

Possible Compromising Threats to Validity

Reactive effect of testing ("guinea pig" effect).

Nonnormality of the distribution of pretest and posttest computer anxiety
scores.

transformation of the data, which is successful only in occasional cases. Since none of the study conclusions is borderline, and since normality is not one of the critical assumptions of analysis of covariance, there is no reason to attempt to refine the analysis further.

The final necessary assumption, homogeneity of variances, is related to the regression assumption of homoscedasticity. That is, the variance of the Ys for a given X is supposed to be the same for all groups and independent of X (the covariate).

Test: Compare the variances of the estimated residuals across treatments (Scheffe, 1959).

Impact: Biased hypothesis test results, depending on the distribution of the variance.

Remedy: Possible transformation of the data.

As before, since this is not a critical assumption, and since there are no borderline hypothesis tests in the laboratory study, there is no reason to attempt to correct for any heteroscedasticity. ANCOVA is not particularly sensitive to violations of the four necessary assumptions, and whatever biases that might result would not affect the conclusions of the study.

Design threats. Flaws in the experimental design or in the procedure of the experiment can threaten the validity of the results. One possible threat is confounding of variables, where unknown effects are at play in addition to the variables that have been isolated and identified. The present study reduces the confounding threat that was present in earlier studies of computer anxiety (Raub, 1981; Weinberg and English, 1983), which ignore an individual's psychological type as a possible correlate. These studies were highly susceptible to the threats of confounding. The present study is, of course, susceptible to this threat, but its possible effects have been minimized by randomization, as discussed earlier.

Mortality threatens pre-post studies when subjects drop out during the treatment period. This is a minimal threat here because of the extremely short period of time between the pretest and posttest.

The most serious design threat in this study is from the reactive effect of testing. The pretest questionnaire will have increased the managers' sensitivity to their thoughts about microcomputers, and the posttest scores could reflect this reactivity. Managers who do not receive a pretest would not be susceptible to this reactive effect, but without the pretest the covariate would not be available and the statistical sensitivity of the test would be greatly reduced. Hence the study design trades off a more sensitive test against the known but limited threat from the reactive effect of testing. The "guinea pig" effect is minimized in the study because the limited capacity of the microcomputer laboratory completely justifies splitting the class into two groups. Campbell and Stanley (1963) emphasize that taking random samples of participants out of intact groups and giving them various treatments is almost certain to be reactive because of the resulting "I'm a guinea pig" attitude. This effect is almost inescapable in laboratory research, and the present study is no exception.

Concise Summary of the Results of the Study

This section summarizes the results of the study in synoptic form. Field study results are in figure 13. Figure 14 presents the summarized results of the pre-post laboratory study.

5

Discussion

Managers' Attitudes toward Microcomputers

An important theme of this study is the potential of microcomputer-based management tools to improve white collar productivity and thus aid organizations in maintaining an edge over their less productive counterparts. Realization of these productivity gains requires that the surprisingly strong resistance of some managers to personal use of microcomputers in management be overcome. Toward that end, a portion of the study was aimed at measuring the collective attitude of managers toward microcomputers, and then discovering the significant correlates of their attitudes. The logic was that knowledge of the correlates of managers' attitudes toward microcomputers would suggest what needs to be changed to overcome their resistance to using microcomputers.

Contrary to many of the reports in the business press, attitudes about using microcomputers in management tasks were found to be highly positive, as reported in chapter 4. The managers polled felt that their use of microcomputers would afford them improved access to information and would not require excessive time, and that microcomputers possessed sufficient computational capability to be of value on problems of a practical scale. Further, they felt that microcomputers would not compromise their managerial image, were not particularly troublesome to use or overly expensive, and would not cause unmanageable compatibility problems because of rapid proliferation. The fact that the sample of managers was randomly selected and contained respondents from a variety of different types of organization who possessed a diversity of educational and experiential backgrounds lends generalizability to the results. Also, there was a high degree of internal consistency in the responses to the attitudes toward microcomputers questions, indicating that the managers tended to respond uniformly to the questions, regardless of the factor to which each individual question pertained. The only departure from this uniformity that is worth noting is that the responses to the questions about compatibility and proliferation indicated that caution is needed, and that organizations should develop policies to prevent the chaos that might result from helter-skelter acquisition of microcomputer hardware and software. On the whole, though, managers have surprisingly uniform and positive attitudes toward their using microcomputers in management tasks.

Some managers' attitudes were more positive than others, though, and this opens the question of what variables seem to correlate with microcomputer attitudes. The study found that the significant correlates of attitudes toward microcomputers are computer anxiety and locus of control.

Correlates of Managers' Attitudes toward Microcomputers

Computer anxiety, as was hypothesized, is an inverse correlate of microcomputer attitudes. Managers with higher levels of computer anxiety had less favorable attitudes toward microcomputers. Although causation cannot be positively established, it seems reasonable that if these managers' computer anxiety could be reduced, an accompanying improvement in microcomputer attitudes and productive use might occur.

Locus of control was a weaker, but still highly significant correlate of attitude toward microcomputers. External locus of control managers were found to have less favorable attitudes about microcomputers. This finding is intuitively appealing and is consistent with other research. External types consider the forces that control their lives to be located outside themselves, and that their destiny is determined by luck and by powerful others. Externals have been found to request less information than internals (Zmud, 1980), and to engage in less information search activity (Lefcourt, 1972; Phares, 1976). It follows that externals would be less likely to use computers. The findings of the present study support this supposition. The correlation between locus of control and microcomputer attitude factor 1 (improved access to information) was $-.1205$ ($p < .045$). This confirms Zmud's findings in that externals, who request less information, will be less impressed by the ability of a microcomputer to improve access to information.

Locus of control is a trait characteristic that is unlikely to change significantly in a person's lifetime (Rotter, 1966). This means that external locus of control managers are likely to retain their less favorable views toward microcomputers over the long term. At the same time, it must be noted that locus of control is a weaker correlate of microcomputer attitudes than is computer anxiety. So a low computer anxious external type might still exhibit a relatively positive attitude toward microcomputers compared to a high computer anxious external type. There is an implication in these findings that externals ought not be chosen for management positions involving frequent interaction with computers, but the implication is fairly weak.

If improvements in white collar productivity depend, in part, on increased management use of microcomputers, which in turn depends on managers' attitudes toward microcomputers, which depends heavily on computer anxiety, then it is important to develop a thorough understanding of the phenomenon of computer anxiety.

Toward a General Theory of Computer Anxiety

There is no general theory of computer anxiety or of, for that matter, anxiety as a broader construct. As discussed in chapter 2, psychologists are not in wide agreement on the definitions of and theory behind stress, tension, anxiety, fear, and phobias. Yet a clear understanding of these phenomena is needed before a more profound comprehension of computer anxiety can be developed. A first step in developing such an understanding is to fabricate a classification scheme for these various psychological constructs. The aim is to unify several fragmented lines of thought on these topics from the psychological literature.

Classifying Reactions to Stress

As was proposed in chapter 2, stress can be regarded as accompanying a situation containing stimuli that arouse uneasiness in a person. This uneasiness can be so subtle as to be subconscious, in which case it can be referred to as tension, a vague feeling of disquiet or restlessness. If the uneasiness that results from stress is somewhat more intense, it becomes conscious. When the individual is fully aware of its presence, then it is referred to as anxiety. Following the work of May (1977), when this uneasiness is the result of a specific, known, and immediate threat, it is called fear. And if that fear is exaggerated relative to the probability that harm will come to the individual, then the fear is termed a phobia. Hence we have a stimulus-response phenomenon. Stress is the stimulus, and the individual reacts at a particular level of intensity to that stress. The level of intensity of that reaction can vary from tension at the low end to phobia at the high end.

Intensity provides one dimension to characterize reactions to stress. Permanence of the reaction is another dimension. Cattell and Scheier (1958) originated the concepts of trait anxiety, a person's basic tendency to be anxious, which does not change appreciably over time, and state anxiety, a transitory condition that varies in intensity and fluctuates over time. These two dimensions characterize a person's reaction to stress, and can be combined to form a two-dimensional map, as shown in figure 15.

Four of the possible reactions to stress are shown in the figure. For example, a highly exaggerated reaction to stress that dies down after the

Figure 15. Classification Map for Reactions to Stress

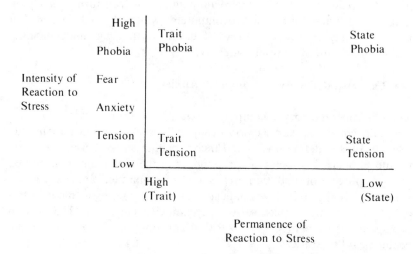

stressor is removed would be classified as a state phobia, whereas a permanent, low grade, almost subconscious reaction to an ongoing stressor would be classified as a trait tension. It is also possible, using this classification scheme, to speak of such reactions as state fear and trait anxiety.

Consciousness and Treatability of Reactions to Stress

This classification scheme can be further enhanced by recognizing that an individual may or may not be conscious of his or her reaction to stress. A permanent, or trait reaction would probably not be noticed simply because it is present all the time. Similarly, a reaction of low intensity, such as tension, might not be particularly noticeable. Figure 16 includes this additional factor as well as a measure of the "treatability" of a particular reaction to stress.

Here it is shown that a reaction that is high in intensity, temporal (thus new and noticeable), or both would be highly conscious, and vice versa. Similarly, a reaction that is low in intensity and temporary would be relatively easy to treat compared to a permanent, high intensity reaction. This graphical construct provides a useful tool for classifying and understanding reactions to stress. Once again, stress is considered to be the stimulus, and the illustration maps the possible range of responses.

Roots and Mechanisms of Computer Anxiety

The preceding diagram effectively characterizes and classifies reactions to stress, but provides no knowledge about the causes or sources of stress or

Figure 16.   Enhanced Classification Map for Reactions to Stress

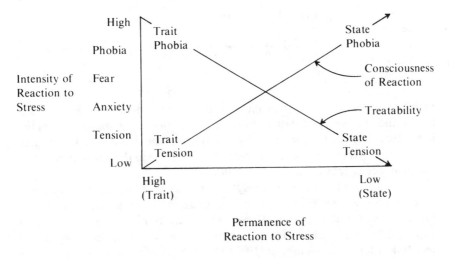

Permanence of
Reaction to Stress

about why different individuals exhibit different reactions to the same stressors. This stimulus-response mechanism can be viewed as shown in figure 17.

There are, in any society, certain general background stressors that are an ongoing part of life, and these give rise to permanent responses that vary from individual to individual, depending upon psychological makeup. These are the kinds of reaction that are usually collectively called trait anxiety. Specific stressors also appear from time to time. The presence of a snake will illicit responses of wildly varying intensity in different individuals, but regardless of the intensity, the reaction disappears in most people when the snake disappears. Math anxiety and computer anxiety fall mainly into this latter class. Anticipation of taking a mathematics test or of interacting with a computer is a specific stress that produces a temporary response, the intensity of which varies with the individual.

The knowledge about the correlates of computer anxiety gained from the study, together with the concept of psychological, knowledge, and operational roots of computer anxiety from chapter 2, can be pieced together with the figure 16 and 17 illustrations to propose a theory of computer anxiety.

Earlier it was suggested that computer anxiety has operational, knowledge, and psychological roots or origins. When confronted with imminent interaction with a computer, fears arise in connection with the mechanics of operating the keyboard, disk drives, or other components (operational fears), in connection with one's possible inability to make the machine perform as desired because of lack of programming skill or an

Figure 17.   Stimulus-Response Model of Stress

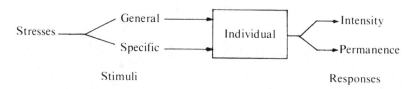

inability to understand why the machine behaves as it does (knowledge-based fears), and in connection with deep-seated psychological characteristics of the individual that elicit vague negative reactions to the computer. These three roots, respectively, represent a hierarchy of reactions to the stress imposed by the prospect of interacting with a computer.

Operational fears are relatively easy to diagnose and treat, knowledge-based fears are somewhat more difficult to assuage, and psychological fears are extremely difficult to understand and treat. Similarly, the operational fears are generally transitory, rising prior to a computer use session and receding afterward. Weinberg (1983) has, for example, used galvanic skin response equipment to verify the state nature of computer anxiety. Knowledge fears are somewhat more persistent, not diminishing until the needed computer knowledge is obtained, while the psychological fears may never diminish unless profound changes occur in the individual's psychological makeup. Thus the psychological fears may be said to be traitlike.

On this basis, then, these three probable origins or roots of negative reactions to computer stress may be mapped onto the intensity-permanence plane, yielding the outcome shown in figure 18.

This diagram graphically summarizes the ideas just presented. When subjected to computer stress because of imminent interaction with a computer, the cyberphobic individual will react at a certain level of intensity and the reaction will have a certain degree of permanence. When the origin of the reaction is operational, the reaction will be statelike, the individual will be highly conscious of the reaction because it differs so from the normal state, and the operational part of the reaction can be easily treated by providing sufficient experience to reduce the operational concerns. At the left side of the map, where the origin of the reaction is psychological, it will be traitlike, the individual may not be particularly conscious of the reaction because it is ongoing, and the psychological part of the reaction will be difficult to treat because treatment requires making fundamental changes in the person's attitudes and beliefs about computers in particular and technology in general.

Admittedly, the preceding construct has been developed inductively. But it is easy to see that there is support for the model of figure 18 in the findings of this and other studies.

Figure 18.   Roots of Negative Reactions to Computer Stress

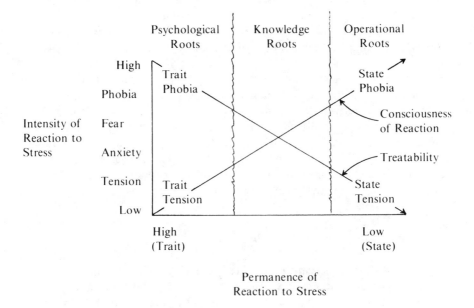

Empirical Support for the Model

Knowledge about the correlates of computer anxiety, while certainly not causal, provides clues about the underlying mechanisms. The present study found computer experience to be the most significant correlate (–.48, $p < .001$). This finding for the population of managers replicates Raub's result for college students of –.47 for males and –.43 for females. It makes good intuitive sense that the more computer experience a person has, the less difficulty he or she will have with the mechanics of operating the equipment, and thus the lower will be the level of the negative reaction that arises from operational problems. Thus the finding that computer experience correlates highly (and inversely) with computer anxiety supports the idea that operational problems are at least part of the source of negative reactions to computers. Experience is easy to impart; thus, the operational roots are seen as easy to treat.

   Knowledge and experience are not the same thing, although they often accompany each other. In the present study, for example, the correlation between computer knowledge and computer experience was .51. Computer knowledge and experience do not always accompany each other, because computer operators generally have high levels of computer experience and somewhat low levels of knowledge about programming languages, system software, and other technical aspects of computing. It is not as easy to impart computer knowledge as it is to provide experience, so negative reactions to computing that arise from lack of knowledge would be expected to be more difficult to treat, justifying the positioning of the knowledge-based reactions to computer stress to the left of the operational reactions in the model of figure 18.

The psychological roots of computer anxiety are related to the individual's fundamental personality, attitudes, and beliefs. A clue to the nature of these beliefs is the finding of all known computer anxiety studies that math anxiety is a significant correlate. In the present study the computer anxiety and math anxiety correlation was .38. Raub (1981) measured the same correlation at .34 for males and .21 for females. This suggests that perhaps computer anxiety and math anxiety are related phenomena, and that an understanding of math anxiety may contribute to an understanding of computer anxiety.

Relating Computer Anxiety to Math Anxiety

Themes (1982) reports that the significant correlates of math anxiety are test anxiety, years of mathematics experience, age, sex, and trait anxiety. Test anxiety clearly has statelike characteristics, the components of which are concern over performance and affective arousal. This finding, coupled with the discovery of mathematics experience as a significant correlate suggests that math anxiety, like computer anxiety, has an "operational" component that would reside at the right end of the intensity-permanence map. Age is probably a spurious correlate because it would relate directly to years of mathematics experience.

At the left end of the map, the fact that trait anxiety is a correlate implies that math anxiety, like computer anxiety, also has a traitlike component. The present study found math anxiety and trait anxiety to be significantly correlated $(.19, p < .023)$. Sex as a math anxiety correlate reflects psychological differences between men and women with regard to mathematics that result from early socialization of females away from scientific and technical endeavors. Thus math anxiety is seen to resemble computer anxiety in that it too has traitlike psychological roots.

Further, the treatments for math anxiety suggest the existence of the same three-level scheme as has been proposed as an explanation of computer anxiety. Themes (1982) studied the relative effectiveness of the three most popular math anxiety treatments: mathematics skills intervention, cognitive-behavior modification, and rational-emotive therapy, and found them to be approximately equally successful. Mathematics skills intervention gives experience (right end of the computer anxiety model), cognitive-behavior modification seeks to impart knowledge and to change patterns of thought about mathematics (center of the model), while rational-emotive therapy seeks to help people dispute their own negative beliefs about mathematics (left end of the computer anxiety model). The fact that each of these treatments brings a degree of success shows that math anxiety, like computer anxiety, is a three-level phenomenon. What is needed, of course, is a treatment that attacks all three levels. This could be expected, given the proposed model, to yield the best treatment success for both math anxiety and computer anxiety.

If, given the argument just developed, math anxiety and computer anxiety are similar phenomena, then they must have common psychological roots. Raub's (1981) study of computer anxiety suggests that technological alienation is a significant cause of computer anxiety, and there is compelling evidence in the present study to confirm the validity of this explanation. Raub arrived at her conclusion based on clinical interviews with computer anxious students, giving the following report.

> The most illuminating question in the interviews was: To what extent do you feel "in touch" or "out of touch" with the advances of computer technology? This question was designed to explore fear of the technological unknown. The computer-anxious students shared a background of alienation or isolation from technology. The computer explosion of the past decade passed by them unnoticed. They described a kind of "Rip Van Winkle" experience: Where have I been during these past 10 years when the computer revolution was taking place? It is from this obliviousness to technology that computer anxiety appears to originate.

Thus the prime psychological root of computer anxiety appears to be that certain people simply do not see themselves as technological types. With this attitude they are defeated before they start. Similarly, math anxious types see mathematics and computers and all the paraphernalia of technology as for somebody else. And this *trait* does not, based on the present study, seem to be related to locus of control or cognitive style. Other more subtle and perhaps unknown psychological variables are at play.

Relationship to Stage Theory

Finally, the theory and model of computer anxiety proposed in the present study are not inconsistent with the stage theory of computer anxiety offered by Raub. Raub suggests that computer anxiety consists of a heterogeneous set of fears, and the present study classifies those fears as operational, knowledge-based, or psychological in origin. Additionally, she says that these fears evolve along an accommodation/assimilation continuum consisting of the five stages of computer alienation, recognized impact of society, impact on personal life, computer accommodation, and assimilation of computer knowledge. The implication here is that treatment of computer anxiety requires a reversal of computer alienation, a change in the resulting attitudes about the impact of computers on society, acceptance of the impact of computers on one's own personal life, acceptance of the need to gain computer skills and knowledge, and finally the acquisition of computer skills and knowledge. These stages can be depicted left to right across the bottom of the proposed computer anxiety model and would be fully consistent with all the features of that model. It is interesting to note, parenthetically, that recognized impact on society is an attitude that would form as a result of one's basic psychological feelings about technology. Accordingly, one would expect high computer anxious individuals to have negative societal impact expectations. The study results confirmed this expectation, yielding a correlation of −.38 between computer anxiety and attitude about impact of computers on society. This finding is wholly consistent with the proposed theoretical framework.

Summarizing the General Theory

Summarizing, the theory of computer anxiety proposed by the present study is that an individual experiences "computer stress" in anticipation of interacting with a computer. This stress has both general and specific components: general in that the present technological world imposes an ongoing background of stress, and specific in that the stress is specific to computing. This idea is depicted in figure 19. Individuals respond to this imposed stress depending upon their psychological makeup, knowledge about computing, and computing experience level. These responses can then be classified according to their intensity and their permanency as shown in the summary diagram of figure 20.

Reactions at the right end of the figure 20 map arise from operational origins and can be treated relatively easily. Reactions in the center stem from knowledge-based origins and are of intermediate difficulty to treat, while those at the left come from psychological roots and are difficult if not impossible to treat. The reactions to computer stress are complex in that they may come from each of the three roots, two of the three, or only one, depending upon the particular individual. The origins of the reactions affect their treatability. For example, a manager's computer anxiety may be 50% psychologically based, 30% knowledge-based, and 20% experience-based. Giving computer experience to this person can only be expected to attack 20% of the problem because the residual anxieties from the other two roots will have gone untreated.

Raub's stages of accommodation-assimilation are given at the bottom of the model in figure 20 to show the correspondence of the stages or sources of computer anxiety with the intensity-permanence map.

Figure 21 gives a tabular summary of the important aspects of the preceding discussion.

Figure 19. Stimulus-Response Model of Computer Anxiety

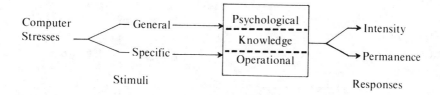

Figure 20. Consolidated Model of Computer Anxiety

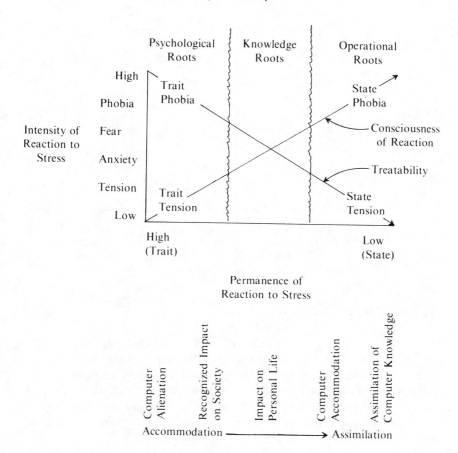

Figure 21.   Tabular Summary of Important Aspects of the
                    Computer Anxiety Phenomenon

Root of Computer Anxiety	Psychological	Knowledge	Operational
Treatment Needed	Change Technological Attitudes and Beliefs	Impart Computer Knowledge	Provide Computer Experience
Ease of Change	Difficult	Moderate	Easy
Time Required to Change	Long	Intermediate	Short
Extent to Which Cause Is Tied to Personality	High	Medium	Low
Indicated by Correlate	Math Anxiety and Trait Anxiety	Impact of Computers on Society	Computer Experience

Real-World Significance of the Results

The findings of this study contradict the popular notions that managers are generally negative about the usefulness of microcomputers and that computer anxiety is an intense and widespread phenomenon. Most managers are, in fact, positive about their personally using microcomputers in support of management decision making, and the incidence of serious cases of computer anxiety in this study is so low as to be insignificant. Where computer anxiety does arise, its intensity is minimal.

Further, the enhanced understanding of the computer anxiety phenomenon that was gained from the study indicates that the problem, when it does exist, is treatable, although not over the short run. Experience with computers is a principal correlate; thus, hands-on microcomputer training can be expected to reduce greatly most anxieties stemming from operational roots. The study results suggest that, while anxieties associated with knowledge and psychological roots may be more difficult to treat, these anxieties are typically quite low compared to the operationally related ones. There is no single, identifiable psychological type of individual that is especially prone to computer anxiety and should thus be excluded from managerial responsibilities. On the contrary, computer anxiety is a relatively innocent phenomenon that can be easily handled, in most cases, by providing experience. The study does show, though, that this experience should be provided over an extended period, and that a brief session will probably not succeed in significantly reducing computer anxiety.

This means that organizations that are trying to indoctrinate managers to microcomputing through short, intensive workshops may be disappointed at the results. Taylor (1983) reports in *Time* that United Technologies, for example, is giving intense three-day training sessions on the IBM PC to each of the 1,100 managers in the firm with an annual salary of $50,000 or more. At the end of the seminar the managers are given the computer, printer, and other accessories to use in whatever fashion they deem appropriate. Yet fewer than 20% of the managers thus trained now use the PC daily in their jobs. Other firms have experienced similar failures. These failures are not surprising given the results of the present study. The hands-on approach being taken by these companies is the right approach, because it effectively imparts the needed microcomputer experience, but the sessions should be offered over a much longer period, in much smaller doses, to be effective. Similarly, the various short-duration high-intensity courses being given to managers by outside consultants and various professional organizations are probably ineffective in significantly reducing computer anxiety.

Finally, it is clear from this and other studies that computer novices should not be introduced to programming until they have become comfortable and competent using high level user-friendly languages such as Lotus 1-2-3 and Multiplan. Early introduction of programming, even using a simple language like BASIC, exerts computer stress in excess, and the resulting negative reactions will present barriers to subsequent learning that may require long periods of time to subside.

Appendix A

Initial Questionnaire on Microcomputer Attitudes

What do you see as the major advantages and disadvantages of your
personally using a microcomputer such as Apple II, TRS-80, IBM PC, etc.,
in your present position?

Please Check One:
Managerial   _____
Professional (Non-managerial)   _____

<u>Advantages</u>

<u>Disadvantages</u>

Appendix B

Item Pool Questionnaire

Attitudes Toward Microcomputers Questionnaire

These questions pertain specifically to microcomputers, such as the IBM
Personal Computer, Radio Shack TRS-80, Commodore 64, etc. The questions probe
your attitudes about your personally using a microcomputer as an aid in your
various management tasks. In responding, please assume that the microcomputer
is not connected to other microcomputers or to a central mainframe computer.
Work quickly, circling the letters that best describe your feeling or reaction
about each statement.

Please check one:

Managerial   _____

Non-management Profession _____

Legend:

Strongly Agree	Agree	Neutral	Disagree	Strongly Disagree
SA	A	N	D	SD

1. I could save time by using a microcomputer   SA   A   N   D   SD

2. I wouldn't use a microcomputer because programming it
   would take too much time.   SA   A   N   D   SD

3. Using a microcomputer would increase my accessability
   to information.   SA   A   N   D   SD

4. I wouldn't use a microcomputer because inputting data
   would take too much time.   SA   A   N   D   SD

5. Using a microcomputer would give me greater control
   over important information.   SA   A   N   D   SD

6. Using microcomputers might cause a problem of inconsistent
   data or duplication of data on the various microcomputers
   within the organization.   SA   A   N   D   SD

7. A microcomputer would give me greater flexibility
   in obtaining information that I need.   SA   A   N   D   SD

8. I wouldn't use a microcomputer because it is too
   time consuming.   SA   A   N   D   SD

9. A microcomputer would give me more timely access to
   needed information.   SA   A   N   D   SD

10. I wouldn't want to have a microcomputer at work because
    it would distract me from my normal job duties.   SA   A   N   D   SD

11. A microcomputer could provide me with information in a
    form exactly tailored to my needs.   SA   A   N   D   SD

12. I wouldn't use a microcomputer because this would be
    clerical in nature.   SA   A   N   D   SD

13. Using a microcomputer to access information would eliminate
    much of the "political massaging" that is currently
    done to information before it reaches me.   SA   A   N   D   SD

14. Using a microcomputer would reduce the time I now spend
    waiting for important information.   SA   A   N   D   SD

15. Using a microcomputer, I could create my own personal
    data base of important information.   SA   A   N   D   SD

16. Using a microcomputer would take too much time from
    my normal duties.   SA   A   N   D   SD

17. I'd like to use a microcomputer because it would force
    me to learn to type.   SA   A   N   D   SD

18. My using a microcomputer would not be desirable because
    I would be the only person who would understand
    how to use the applications that I programmed.   SA   A   N   D   SD

19. A microcomputer would be a valuable aid to me in
    organizing my work.   SA   A   N   D   SD

20. Using a microcomputer would involve too much time
    doing mechanical operations (programming, inputting data,
    etc.) to allow sufficient time for managerial analysis.   SA   A   N   D   SD

21. Using a microcomputer would reduce my dependency on
    outside information sources.   SA   A   N   D   SD

22. I wouldn't want a microcomputer because my office is
    already too crowded.   SA   A   N   D   SD

23. Using a microcomputer could provide me with information
    that would lead to better decisions.   SA   A   N   D   SD

24. I wouldn't encourage my company to acquire microcomputers
    because of the high purchase cost of the machine
    and its software.   SA   A   N   D   SD

25. I'd like to use a microcomputer because it
    would give me an opportunity to learn to program.   SA   A   N   D   SD

26. I wouldn't use a microcomputer because it is not a
    secure way to store important information.   SA   A   N   D   SD

27. I'd like to use a microcomputer because it would give
    me an opportunity to learn more about computers.   SA   A   N   D   SD

28. I wouldn't want a microcomputer because it would take
    too long to learn to use.   SA A N D SD

29. I'd like to use a microcomputer because it would
    eliminate all calculation errors.   SA A N D SD

30. I wouldn't want to use a microcomputer because it
    would reduce my interaction with people.   SA A N D SD

31. Using a microcomputer would give me the capability to
    generate reports quickly and in varied formats.   SA A N D SD

32. Using a microcomputer would result in a tendency
    to overdesign simple tasks.   SA A N D SD

33. Using a microcomputer would permit me to do
    significant amounts of my work at home.   SA A N D SD

34. A microcomputer wouldn't benefit me because few management
    issues are answerable in black and white.   SA A N D SD

35. Using a microcomputer would be desirable because of
    its low maintenance cost.   SA A N D SD

36. I wouldn't use a microcomputer because any
    question it could answer should be answerable
    at a lower level in the organization.   SA A N D SD

37. I'd like to use a microcomputer because of the word
    processing capability it would give me.   SA A N D SD

38. I wouldn't want a microcomputer because I would not be
    able to delegate the routine data lock-up tasks
    which I now delegate.   SA A N D SD

39. I'd like to use a microcomputer because of the fast
    statistical analysis capabilities it would provide.   SA A N D SD

40. Using a microcomputer might cause me to answer queries too
    quickly, without applying sufficient judgement.   SA A N D SD

41. Using a microcomputer would give me more
    time for the professional aspects of my job.   SA A N D SD

42. A microcomputer would waste my time if no direction were
    provided by the company on policies for its use.   SA A N D SD

43. Using a microcomputer would allow for eventual replacement
    of the on-line applications that presently run on
    the mainframe computer.   SA A N D SD

44. I wouldn't use a microcomputer because of its "toy" image. SA A N D SD

45. I'd like using a microcomputer because I could
    write my own applications.   SA A N D SD

46. I wouldn't favor using a microcomputer because there would be a tendency to use it even when it was more consuming than manual methods.   SA   A   N   D   SD

47. I'd like to use a microcomputer because there are many application packages commercially available.   SA   A   N   D   SD

48. I'd discourage my company from using micro-computers because of the redundant capabilities that would result if too many were purchased.   SA   A   N   D   SD

49. By using a microcomputer, I'd spend less time translating my information wants and needs to others.   SA   A   N   D   SD

50. I'd hesitate to acquire a microcomputer for my use at work because of the difficulty of integrating it with existing information systems.   SA   A   N   D   SD

51. Using a microcomputer would enable me to learn more about information systems in general.   SA   A   N   D   SD

52. A microcomputer would be of no use to me because of its small storage capacity.   SA   A   N   D   SD

53. Using a microcomputer would give me the capability for faster analysis of information.   SA   A   N   D   SD

54. A potential problem with microcomputer use by managers at work is the proliferation of incompatible programs within an organization.   SA   A   N   D   SD

55. A microcomputer would be of use to me because it would allow for faster production of charts and graphs.   SA   A   N   D   SD

56. I couldn't make effective use of a microcomputer unless it were connected to the mainframe computer.   SA   A   N   D   SD

57. A microcomputer would be useful to me for keeping my appointment calendar and for providing "tickler" reminders about deadlines and due dates.   SA   A   N   D   SD

58. I'd like to have a microcomputer because they are so easy to use.   SA   A   N   D   SD

59. I'd discourage my company from acquiring microcomputers because of the difficulty of getting service.   SA   A   N   D   SD

60. I'd like to use a microcomputer because it is oriented to user needs.   SA   A   N   D   SD

61. I'd discourage my company from acquiring microcomputers because most application packages would need to be modified before they could be useful in our specific situation.   SA   A   N   D   SD

62. If I as a manager get a microcomputer, then everyone else in the organization will want one.   SA   A   N   D   SD

63. I wouldn't use a microcomputer because I can't type.   SA   A   N   D   SD

64. A microcomputer would be of no use to me because of its limited computing power.   SA   A   N   D   SD

65. I wouldn't use a microcomputer because I would not personally enjoy using it.   SA   A   N   D   SD

66. A microcomputer would be of no use to me because of the limited availability of application program packages.   SA   A   N   D   SD

67. I'd discourage my company from acquiring microcomputers because of the high cost of application software packages.   SA   A   N   D   SD

68. Microcomputers are primarily just toys, much as video games, so they can't be of much real use to managers.   SA   A   N   D   SD

69. If I knew how to use one, I'd like to have a microcomputer on my desk.   SA   A   N   D   SD

70. A microcomputer would be of no value to me because I don't know how to write computer programs.   SA   A   N   D   SD

71. If I personally used a microcomputer at work, it would damage the managerial image that I want to project.   SA   A   N   D   SD

72. Microcomputers have far too little computing capability to be useful to managers in real life business situations.   SA   A   N   D   SD

73. Microcomputers can provide valuable assistance to managers in tasks such as budget planning and preparation, tax planning and preparation, and others.   SA   A   N   D   SD

74. If I knew how to use one and one were available, I'd use a microcomputer at work.   SA   A   N   D   SD

75. Microcomputers don't belong in managers' offices.   SA   A   N   D   SD

76. I'd like to learn about ways that microcomputers can be used to aid in management tasks.   SA   A   N   D   SD

77. I think that using a microcomputer at work would improve my productivity.   SA   A   N   D   SD

78. I think it would be fun to use a microcomputer at work.   SA   A   N   D   SD

79. My boss would look favorably on my using a microcomputer at work.   SA   A   N   D   SD

80. I'd encourage any managers who report to me to learn about and use microcomputers at work.   SA   A   N   D   SD

81. My organization encourages its managers to personally use microcomputers at work.   SA   A   N   D   SD

Appendix C

Factor Loadings after Varimax Rotation

Varimax Rotated Factor Matrix

Item	1	2	3	4	5	6
1	0.39398	-0.16618	-0.40416	-0.47669	-0.18184	-0.09364
2	-0.20007	0.71831	0.26310	0.27847	0.08593	0.08593
3	0.41970	-0.42231	-0.41889	-0.45401	0.03099	0.07845
4	-0.46014	0.60940	0.46326	0.25838	-0.23789	0.13626
5	0.65379	0.09293	-0.19494	0.04085	0.17273	-0.23454
6	-0.30512	-0.15773	0.28585	0.09035	0.17713	0.08579
7	0.47507	-0.20796	-0.16854	-0.07318	0.25712	0.12400
8	-0.20690	0.60377	0.46747	0.06110	-0.26535	-0.13878
9	0.56164	-0.04534	-0.25844	0.04806	0.03936	-0.17891
10	-0.41951	0.78366	0.01681	0.04780	-0.14388	0.08625
11	0.69456	-0.16236	0.16748	-0.23783	0.31380	-0.06614
12	-0.02349	0.55478	0.19551	0.71008	-0.09745	0.01657
13	0.38456	-0.16531	-0.24948	-0.36330	-0.07334	-0.21119
14	0.46369	-0.20094	-0.43428	-0.31383	0.06794	-0.19834
15	0.90543	-0.10414	-0.09783	0.05694	-0.03544	0.10280
16	-0.31644	0.51010	-0.06718	-0.03657	-0.47728	0.23526
17	0.22392	0.46882	0.03849	0.07128	-0.29903	-0.36850
18	0.20836	0.31712	0.55290	0.41406	0.20520	0.10710
19	0.82678	-0.32581	-0.16871	-0.20961	0.04170	-0.07421
20	-0.20771	0.36593	0.44235	0.17644	-0.47604	0.26992
21	0.04053	0.00087	-0.10110	0.08128	0.01067	-0.00737
22	-0.46720	0.46000	0.22926	0.09500	-0.15239	0.25621
23	0.68848	-0.20621	-0.31577	-0.04243	0.15042	-0.25275
24	-0.41025	0.22214	0.32275	0.07734	-0.65142	-0.19897
25	-0.08827	-0.08514	0.11104	-0.15802	0.12910	0.26226
26	-0.10292	0.01562	0.64680	0.21925	0.20083	-0.11458
27	0.30463	-0.63337	-0.36090	0.08909	-0.02217	-0.08852
28	-0.11631	0.71335	0.17480	0.20866	0.07482	0.03568
29	-0.02610	-0.17878	-0.39442	-0.36314	0.03234	-0.04902
30	0.07502	0.80053	-0.12271	0.06583	0.17537	0.18809
31	0.85385	-0.20007	-0.13772	0.09516	-0.05321	-0.14347
32	-0.85223	0.51254	0.12340	0.67398	-0.03799	0.11696
33	0.06876	0.03300	0.01944	-0.62655	-0.12794	-0.24724
34	-0.30005	0.36467	0.01247	0.35691	-0.33914	0.29301
35	0.09941	-0.07611	-0.18638	0.42376	0.14593	-0.22498
36	-0.37887	0.83957	-0.07570	0.08411	-0.11636	-0.14106
37	0.30979	- .15608	0.08274	-0.79615	0.15693	0.12118
38	0.21407	0.56573	0.12061	0.66946	-0.02320	0.13772
39	0.09363	-0.35433	-0.07689	-0.08102	0.24224	-0.11521
40	0.07854	-0.02035	0.09760	-0.01666	0.12812	0.02007
41	0.23496	-0.42425	-0.28337	-0.13502	0.01285	-0.18392
42	-0.65948	0.28593	0.42631	0.14899	0.03245	0.10013
43	0.31945	0.05657	0.03250	0.30760	0.15801	-0.01385
44	-0.61159	0.30484	0.40173	0.22713	-0.07844	0.01460
45	0.02130	-0.41696	-0.18064	-0.01503	0.03503	0.17001
46	0.05887	0.41789	0.62433	-0.08576	-0.13264	0.41105
47	0.30883	0.15495	-0.32213	-0.06980	0.18652	0.01117
48	-0.82534	0.00231	0.37692	0.04939	-0.11673	0.00640
49	0.12348	0.12329	-0.41607	0.14126	0.12883	-0.19594
50	-0.23003	0.36823	0.45172	-0.14457	-0.21615	0.30951

51	-0.13056	-0.06332	0.07982	-0.00868	0.05788	-0.04566
52	-0.41525	0.11022	0.65473	0.19447	0.01498	0.28956
53	0.55098	0.11082	-0.31317	0.00026	0.08152	0.01251
54	0.13143	0.12727	0.10915	0.21295	-0.08171	0.88582
55	0.54748	-0.00949	-0.20363	0.27822	0.26822	-0.34353
56	0.10131	0.27042	0.67617	-0.03882	-0.21565	0.31422
57	0.49661	-0.00380	-0.18198	0.12589	0.49610	-0.16438
58	0.30628	-0.61777	-0.30262	-0.06515	0.05092	-0.33929
59	-0.57847	0.50119	0.45312	-0.07235	0.08008	-0.02772
60	0.40513	0.20799	-0.78185	-0.01741	-0.14452	0.00441
61	-0.40093	0.07753	0.16086	0.05390	-0.18929	0.75703
62	-0.04834	0.30394	-0.08968	0.15814	0.22208	0.57874
63	-0.09950	0.83935	0.01523	0.17417	-0.18081	0.12114
64	-0.41815	0.10873	0.85880	-0.00433	-0.12611	0.02026
65	-0.63675	0.35791	0.17807	-0.03646	0.00710	-0.28821
66	-0.17447	- .13587	0.81711	-0.21614	0.04882	0.01316
67	-0.28646	0.09539	0.73983	0.08031	-0.07556	0.01249
68	-0.50292	0.06806	0.69289	0.12093	-0.05956	-0.14952
69	0.60029	-0.51688	-0.06852	-0.00387	0.26894	0.30580
70	-0.42343	0.37432	0.07614	0.39083	-0.22665	0.09139
71	0.12181	0.23730	-0.03439	0.78802	-0.31776	0.24088
72	-0.59971	-0.11791	0.57592	0.12962	-0.27743	0.12377
73	0.25778	-0.46208	-0.53402	-0.20135	0.16692	-0.07751
74	0.83408	-0.10506	-0.22330	-0.05480	0.17992	0.11419
75	-0.24223	0.57012	0.55520	0.22176	-0.28573	0.00992
76	0.44285	-0.20155	-0.09587	0.12507	0.19625	0.12494
77	0.78883	-0.35913	-0.11968	-0.04092	0.16400	-0.16999
78	0.68091	-0.18818	-0.20422	-0.17352	0.33815	0.04599
80*	0.20076	-0.18746	-0.07093	-0.22566	0.89411	-0.13806

*Items 79 and 81 were excluded from the factor analysis.

Appendix D

Consolidated Questionnaire Battery: Computer Attitudes Survey

<u>Computer Attitudes Questionnaire</u>

This questionnaire has been carefully and scientifically designed to measure your attitudes toward computers and some basic aspects of your personality.

At first glance there appear to be a large number of questions, but preliminary tests indicate that most people need only 25 minutes to finish. Please answer <u>all</u> the questions. Partially completed questionnaires are of no value to us.

The survey is anonymous. Please don't put your name anywhere on the questionnaire.

Thank you for your cooperation.

This first group of questions pertains specifically to microcomputers, such as the IBM Personal Computer, Radio Shack TRS-80, Commodore 64, Apple II, etc. The questions probe your attitudes about <u>your personally using</u> a microcomputer as an aid in your various management tasks. In answering, please assume that the microcomputer is sitting on your desk and is not attached to any equipment other than its own printer and monitor. Work quickly, circling the letters that best describe your feeling about or reaction to each statement.

Legend:

Strongly Agree	Agree	Undecided	Disagree	Strongly Disagree
SA	A	U	D	SD

1. A microcomputer would give me more timely access to needed information. SA A U D SD

2. I wouldn't use a microcomputer because programming it would take too much time. SA A U D SD

3. A microcomputer would be of no use to me because of its small storage capacity. SA A U D SD

4. I wouldn't use a microcomputer because this would be clerical in nature. SA A U D SD

5. Using a microcomputer would take too much time from my normal duties. SA A U D SD

6. I would hesitate to acquire a microcomputer for my use at work because of the difficulty of integrating it with existing information systems. SA A U D SD

7. A microcomputer could provide me with information in a form exactly tailored to my needs. SA A U D SD

8. I wouldn't use a microcomputer because inputting data would take too much time. SA A U D SD

9. A microcomputer would be of no use to me because of its limited computing power. SA A U D SD

10. Using a microcomputer would result in a tendency to overdesign simple tasks. SA A U D SD

11. Using a microcomputer would involve too much time doing mechanical operations (programming, inputting data, etc.) to allow sufficient time for managerial analysis. SA A U D SD

12. A potential problem with microcomputer use by managers at work is the proliferation of incompatible programs within an organization. SA A U D SD

13. Using a microcomputer, I could create my own personal database of important information. SA A U D SD

14. I wouldn't use a microcomputer because it is too time consuming. SA A U D SD

15. Microcomputers are primarily just toys, such as video games, so they can't be of much real use to managers.   SA   A   U   D   SD

16. I wouldn't want a microcomputer because I would not be able to delegate the routine data look-up tasks which I now delegate.   SA   A   U   D   SD

17. I wouldn't encourage my company to acquire micro-computers because of the high purchase cost of the machine and its software.   SA   A   U   D   SD

18. I would discourage my company from acquiring microcomputers because most application packages would need to be modified before they would be useful in our specific situation.   SA   A   U   D   SD

19. Using a microcomputer could provide me with information that would lead to better decisions.   SA   A   U   D   SD

20. I wouldn't want a microcomputer because it would take too long to learn to use.   SA   A   U   D   SD

21. Microcomputers have far too little computing capability to be useful to managers in real life business situations.   SA   A   U   D   SD

22. If I personally used a microcomputer at work, it would damage the managerial image that I want to project.   SA   A   U   D   SD

23. I would encourage any managers who report to me to learn about and use microcomputers at work.   SA   A   U   D   SD

24. If I as a manager get a microcomputer, then everyone else in the organization will want one.   SA   A   U   D   SD

Please respond to this next group of questions with regard to computers in general, and not just to microcomputers. Circle the choice that best describes your feeling about or reaction to each statement, and continue to work quickly.

25. I am confident that I could learn computer skills.   SA   A   U   D   SD

26. I am unsure of my ability to learn a computer programming language.   SA   A   U   D   SD

27. I will be able to keep up with the important technological advances of computers.   SA   A   U   D   SD

28. I feel apprehensive about using a computer terminal.   SA   A   U   D   SD

29. If given the opportunity to use a computer, I'm afraid that I might damage it in some way.   SA   A   U   D   SD

30. I have avoided computers because they are unfamiliar to me.   SA A U D SD

31. I hesitate to use a computer for fear of making mistakes that I cannot correct.   SA A U D SD

32. I am unsure of my ability to interpret a computer printout.   SA A U D SD

33. I have difficulty understanding most technological matters.   SA A U D SD

34. Computer terminology sounds like confusing jargon to me.   SA A U D SD

35. Human beings will misuse the power of the computer.   SA A U D SD

36. Computers are changing the world too rapidly.   SA A U D SD

37. Our country relies too much on computers.   SA A U D SD

38. Computers dehumanize society by treating everyone as a number.   SA A U D SD

39. In the future, power will be concentrated in the hands of the technology elite.   SA A U D SD

40. Computers have the potential to control our lives.   SA A U D SD

41. Computers are beneficial aids to modern society.   SA A U D SD

42. Computers will create more jobs than they will eliminate.   SA A U D SD

The following statements refer to your personal experiences with mathematics. Please circle the response that best describes your feeling about or reaction to each statement.

43. Math doesn't scare me at all.   SA A U D SD

44. Mathematics usually makes me feel uncomfortable and nervous.   SA A U D SD

45. It wouldn't bother me at all to take more math courses.   SA A U D SD

46. Mathematics makes me feel uncomfortable, restless, irritable, and impatient.   SA A U D SD

47. I haven't usually worried about being able to solve math problems.   SA A U D SD

48. I get a sinking feeling when I think of trying hard math problems.   SA A U D SD

49. I almost never got shook up during a math test.   SA A U D SD

50. My mind goes blank and I am unable to think clearly
    when working mathematics problems.   SA A U D SD

51. I was usually at ease during math tests.   SA A U D SD

52. A math test would scare me.   SA A U D SD

53. I was usually at ease in math class.   SA A U D SD

54. Mathematics makes me feel uneasy and confused.   SA A U D SD

The next group of questions explores the way in which certain important events
in our society affect different people. Each item consists of a pair of
statements, and next to each statement are the words "Very Close" and
"Slightly Close." First, decide which of the two statements you personally
believe to be the case, then circle "Very Close" if the statement is very
close to your personal feeling, or "Slightly Close" if the statement is only
slightly close to your personal feeling. This means that you will have
circled one of the four choices associated with each question. Be sure to
respond based on what you actually believe rather than on how you think you
should respond or on what you would like to be true. This is a measure of
personal belief: obviously there are no right or wrong answers. Please
answer the items carefully, but do not spend too much time on any one item.
In some instances, you may discover that you believe both statements or
neither one. In such cases, be sure to select the one choice you
strongly believe to be true as far as you are concerned. Also, try to respond
independently when making your choice; do not be influenced by your previous
choices. The first item is already marked as an example.

XX. Very Close   Slightly Close   One of the major reasons why we have
                                         wars is because people don't take
                                         enough interest in politics.

     Very Close   Slightly Close   There will always be wars, no matter
                                         how hard people try to prevent them.

55. Very Close   Slightly Close   Many of the unhappy things in peoples'
                                         lives are partly due to bad luck.

     Very Close   Slightly Close   Peoples' misfortunes result from the
                                         mistakes they make.

56. Very Close   Slightly Close   In the long run, people get the respect
                                         they deserve in this world.

     Very Close   Slightly Close   Unfortunately, an individual's worth
                                         often passes unrecognized no matter
                                         how hard he tries.

57. Very Close   Slightly Close   Without the right breaks, one cannot
                                         be an effective leader.

     Very Close   Slightly Close   Capable people who fail to become leaders
                                         have not taken advantage of their
                                         opportunities.

58. Very Close   Slightly Close   Becoming a success is a matter of hard work; luck has little or nothing to do with it.

    Very Close   Slightly Close   Getting a good job depends mainly on being in the right place at the right time.

59. Very Close   Slightly Close   What happens to me is my own doing.

    Very Close   Slightly Close   Sometimes I feel that I don't have enough control over the direction my life is taking.

60. Very Close   Slightly Close   When I make plans, I am almost certain that I can make them work.

    Very Close   Slightly Close   It is not always wise to plan too far ahead, because many things turn out to be a matter of good or bad fortune anyway.

61. Very Close   Slightly Close   In my case, getting what I want has little or nothing to do with luck.

    Very Close   Slightly Close   Many times we might just as well decide what to do by flipping a coin.

62. Very Close   Slightly Close   Who gets to be boss often depends on who was lucky to be in the right place first.

    Very Close   Slightly Close   Getting people to do the right thing depends upon ability; luck has little or nothing to do with it.

63. Very Close   Slightly Close   Most people don't realize the extent to which their lives are controlled by accidental happenings.

    Very Close   Slightly Close   There is really no such thing as "luck."

64. Very Close   Slightly Close   In the long run, the bad things that happen to us are balanced by the good ones.

    Very Close   Slightly Close   Most misfortunes are the result of lack of ability, ignorance, laziness, or all three.

65. Very Close   Slightly Close   Many times I feel that I have little influence over the things that happen to me.

    Very Close   Slightly Close   It is impossible for me to believe that luck or chance plays an important role in my life.

The next group of questions are designed to measure the way in which you have developed in your approach to dealing with work related problems. The answer you choose for any item is neither right nor wrong. It simply helps to point out the way you study problems. Listed below are a number of statements. Each represents a personal opinion about various activities or events. You will probably agree with some and disagree with others. We are interested in the extent to which you agree or disagree with each statement. Read each item carefully, then circle the choice that corresponds to your opinion for that question. First opinions are usually best in such matters. If you find that the answers do not adequately indicate your personal opinion, use the one that comes <u>closest</u> to the way you feel.

Legend:

Strongly Agree SA	Slightly Agree A	Slightly Disagree D	Strongly Disagree SD

66. In my daily work I usually plan so that I am not pressured for time in meeting a deadline   SA   A   D   SD

67. If asked a few days before a holiday what you were going to do that day, you would have to wait and see.   SA   A   D   SD

68. Following a schedule cramps me.   SA   A   D   SD

69. The idea of making a list of what I should get done over the weekend appeals to me.   SA   A   D   SD

70. I am more of a "planner" than a "doer."   SA   A   D   SD

71. I like to arrange my dates and parties some distance ahead.   SA   A   D   SD

72. When starting a big project that is due in a week, I like to list the things to be done and the order of doing them.   SA   A   D   SD

73. I can <u>more easily</u> cope with set routine than constant change.   SA   A   D   SD

74. I am a spontaneous person.   SA   A   D   SD

75. I am at my best when following a plan.   SA   A   D   SD

76. When writing a report, I just sit down and start writing.   SA   A   D   SD

77. "Scheduled" has <u>more</u> appeal to me than "unplanned."   SA   A   D   SD

78. Where I live I seldom keep my letters and other personal things neatly arranged and filed.   SA   A   D   SD

79. I am at my best when dealing with the unexpected.   SA   A   D   SD

80. The idea of making a list of what I should get
    done over the weekend depresses me.   SA   A   D   SD

81. When there is an unfamiliar special job to be done,
    I like to find out what is necessary as I go along
    rather than attempting to organize it carefully
    before starting.   SA   A   D   SD

82. If asked a few days before a holiday what you were
    going to do that day, you would be able to tell
    pretty well.   SA   A   D   SD

This next group contains statements which people have used to describe
themselves. Read each statement and then circle the letters that indicate
how you <u>generally</u> feel. Do not spend too much time on any one statement.
but give the answer which seems to describe how you generally feel.*

Legend:

Almost Always	Often	Sometimes	Never
A	0	S	N

83. I feel pleasant   A   0   S   N

. . . .

86. I wish that I could be as happy as others seem to be. A   0   S   N

. . . .

90. I feel that difficulties are piling up so that I
    cannot overcome them.   A   0   S   N

. . . .

99. Some unimportant thought runs through my head and
    bothers me.   A   0   S   N

. . . .

102. I get in a state of tension or turmoil as I think
     over my recent concerns and interests.   A   0   S   N

The next questions are multiple choice and pertain to your knowledge about
computers in general. Please circle the choice that you believe to be the
best answer to each question, or circle "d" for "Don't know."

103. CPU stands for

    a. Computer Processor Understanding.
    b. Computer Processing Unit.
    c. Central Processing Unit.
    d. Don't know.

---

*Only sample items are shown for this group. The rows
of ellipsis points indicate missing items.

104. Information is actually internally stored and manipulated by a computer in _____ form.

    a. decimal
    b. character
    c. binary
    d. Don't know.

105. Early computers used what type of processing?

    a. Batch
    b. Interactive
    c. Virtual
    d. Don't know.

106. An example of computer software is

    a. computer printer.
    b. computer program.
    c. computer operator.
    d. Don't know.

107. Translation of high level languages into machine language is done by a(an)

    a. compiler
    b. assembler
    c. encoder
    d. Don't know.

108. Which of the following is not a programming language?

    a. DIFT
    b. ADA
    c. LISP
    d. Don't know.

109. Which of these is not a programming language?

    a. COBOL
    b. SIMPLEX
    c. FORTRAN
    d. Don't know.

110. Which of the following is considered a secondary storage device?

    a. Core memory
    b. Punched cards
    c. Disk
    d. Don't know.

111. A computer architecture that permits the real memory to act as if it is larger than it really is is called

    a. phantom memory.
    b. virtual memory.
    c. variable memory.
    d. Don't know.

112. A concept that revolutionized the practice of computer programming is

     a. Optimal-Path Programming.
     b. Structured Programming.
     c. User-Centered Programming.
     d. Don't know.

The next six questions assess your level of actual experience in working with computers. Please circle the choice that corresponds to your years of experience in each of the categories.

113. I've used printouts produced by someone else for:	Zero Years	Less Than 1 Year	1 - 3 Years	More Than 3 Years
114. I've operated a computer terminal as part of an already existing system, such as a capital budgeting system for:	Zero Years	Less Than 1 Year	1 - 3 Years	More Than 3 Years
115. I've participated in the non-technical design of computer information systems for:	Zero Years	Less Than 1 Year	1 - 3 Years	More Than 3 Years
116. I've participated in the technical design of computer information systems for:	Zero Years	Less Than 1 Year	1 - 3 Years	More Than 3 Years
117. I've written programs in a language such as FORTRAN, COBOL, PL/1, etc., for:	Zero Years	Less Than 1 Year	1 - 3 Years	More Than 3 Years
118. I've earned my living with my knowledge of computer hardware and software for:	Zero Years	Less Than 1 Year	1 - 3 Years	More Than 3 Years

These last few questions are needed so that we can develop a demographic profile of the group of managers who responded to the questionnaire.

119. Please indicate your functional area: (circle one)

     Accounting   Finance   General Management   Information Systems

     Manufacturing/Production   Marketing   Purchasing   R and D

     Sales   Transportation/Traffic   Warehouse/Shipping/Receiving

     Other_____

120. What is the nature of your organization's business? (circle one)

     Manufacturing   Service   Merchandising   Government   Military

     Other_____

121. Please circle your highest level of education and your college major
      if appropriate.

Some   High   Some   Bachelor's   Some   Master's   Post-Master
High   School   College   Degree   Graduate   Degree   Work
School   Graduate   Work

Accounting   Finance   Marketing   Production   Management

Operations Research   Computers   Engineering   Liberal Arts

Fine Arts   Other_____   Not Applicable

122. What are your approximate total years of work experience, excluding
      incidental employment such as college or summer jobs, etc.?_____

123. Please give your age._____

124. Circle your sex: Male   Female

125. What is your current job title?_____

Bibliography

Ahl, D.H. 1976. Survey of public attitudes toward computers in society. In *The best of creative computing,* vol. 1, ed. D.H. Ahl, pp. 77–79. Morristown, N.J.: Creative Computing Press.

Atiqullah, M. 1964. The robustness of covariance analysis in a one-way classification. *Biometrika* 51:365–72.

Bander, R.S.; Russell, R.K.; and Zamostny, K.P. 1982. A comparison of cue-controlled relaxation and study skills counseling in the treatment of mathematics anxiety. *Journal of Educational Psychology* 74:96–103.

Barkin, S. 1974. *An investigation into some factors affecting information system utilization.* Unpublished Ph.D. dissertation, University of Minnesota. 1974.

Barnett, R., and Baruch, G. 1978. *The competent woman, perspectives on development.* New York: Irvington Publishers.

Benbow, B.L. 1979. Math avoidance and pursuit of fantasy careers. American Educational Research Association Meeting, San Francisco.

Bereiter, C. 1963. Some persisting dilemmas in the measurement of change. In *Problems in measuring change,* ed. C.W. Harris. Madison, Wis.: University of Wisconsin Press.

Betz, N. 1978. Prevalence, distribution, and correlates of math anxiety in college students. *Journal of Counseling Psychology* 25:441–48.

Bralove, M. 1983. Computer anxiety hits middle management. *Wall Street Journal,* March 29, 1983.

Brenner, C. 1953. An addendum to Freud's theory of anxiety. *International Journal of Psycho-Analysis* 34:18–24.

Broedling, L.A. 1975. Relationship of internal-external control to work motivation and performance in an expectancy model. *Journal of Applied Psychology* 60:65–70.

Brush, L.R. 1981. Some thoughts for teachers on mathematics anxiety. *The Arithmetic Teacher* 29:37–39.

Campbell, D.T., and Stanley, J.C. 1963. *Experimental and quasi-experimental designs for research.* Chicago: Rand McNally and Co.

Caplan, R.D., and Jones, K.W. 1975. Effects of work load, role ambiguity, and type A personality on anxiety, depression, and heart rate. *Journal of Applied Psychology* 60(6).

Cattell, R.B., and Scheier, I.H. 1958. The nature of anxiety: a review of thirteen multivariate analyses comprising 814 variables. *Psychological Reports* 4:351–88.

———. 1963. *Handbook for the IPAT anxiety scale.* 2d ed. Champaign, Ill.: Institute for Personality and Ability Testing.

CBS Inc. 1982. Transcript of CBS Evening News with Dan Rather, Charles Osgood interview with Dr. Sanford Weinberg, September 24, 1982.

Coli, Steve. 1986. "New category of phobics fears computers." Reprinted from *Washington Post* in *Akron Beacon Journal,* January 6, p. B5.

Conover, W.J. 1980. *Practical nonparametric statistics.* New York: John Wiley and Sons.

Davis, G.B. 1974. *Management information systems: conceptual foundations, structure and development.* Tokyo: McGraw Hill.

DeSanctis, G. 1982. An examination of an expectancy theory model of decision support system use. Proceedings of the SMIS.

Dickson, G.; Senn, J.A.; and Chervany, N. 1977. Research in management information systems: the Minnesota Experiments. *Management Science* 23:913-23.

Dowling, D.M. 1978. The development of a mathematics confidence scale and its application in the study of confidence in women college students. Unpublished doctoral dissertation, The Ohio State University.

Elashoff, J.D. 1969. Analysis of covariance: A delicate instrument. *American Educational Research Journal* 6:383-401.

Elkins, G.R., and Cochran, S.W. 1978. Internal and external locus of control as determinants of decision making in a game of skill. *Psychological Reports* 42(3), Part 2.

Ellis, A., and Abrahams, E. 1978. *Brief psychotherapy in medical and health practice.* New York: Springer Publishing.

Evans, S.H., and Anastasio, E.J. 1968. Misuse of analysis of covariance when treatment effect and covariate are confounded. *Psychological Bulletin* 69:225-34.

Fear of trying: some executives resist the trend toward automation. 1983. *Wall Street Journal,* March 22, 1983, p. 1.

Feldt, L.S. 1958. A comparison of three experimental designs employing a concomitant variable. *Psychometrika* 23:335-53.

Fennema, E., and Sherman, J.A. 1976. Fennema-Sherman mathematics attitude scales, instruments. Designed to measure attitudes toward the learning of mathematics by females and males. *Journal for Research in Mathematics Education* 7:324-26.

Fennema, E.; Wolleat, P.L.; Pedro, J.D.; and Becker, A.D. 1981. Increasing women's participation in mathematics: an intervention study. *Journal for Research in Mathematics Education* 12:3-4.

Fox, L.H.; Brody, K.; and Tobin, D., eds. 1980. *Women and the mathematical mystique.* Baltimore, Md.: The Johns Hopkins University Press.

French, J.R.P., and Caplan, R.D. 1972. Organizational stress and individual strain. In *The failure of success,* ed. A.J. Marrow. New York: AMACOM.

Freud, S. 1959 (originally published, 1926). *Inhibitions, symptoms, and anxiety.* London: Hogarth Press.

Healion, J.V. 1983. Compuphobia isn't terminal. UPI article in *Youngstown Vindicator,* April 3, 1983.

Huck, S., and McLean, R.A. 1975. Using a repeated measures ANOVA to analyze data from a pretest-posttest design: a potentially confusing task. *Psychological Bulletin* 82:511-18.

Hull, C., and Nie, N.H. 1981. SPSS Update 7-9. New York: McGraw-Hill Book Company.

Inman, V. 1983. Learning how to use computers is frightening experience for many. *Wall Street Journal,* April 12, 1983, p. 1.

Intel Corp. introduces a computer system aimed at managers. 1982. *Wall Street Journal,* October 7, 1982, p. 38.

James, F. 1982. Got vertigo over video displays? Maybe it's a case of cyberphobia. *Wall Street Journal,* June 8, 1982, p. 37.

Jung, C.G. 1923. *Psychological types.*

Junghans, B.J. 1980. Math anxiety, math avoidance, participation in math: a summary of research curriculum, recommendations for career education. ERIC Document Reproduction Service No. ED 194 346.

Keppel, G. 1973. *Design and analysis: a researcher's handbook.* Englewood Cliffs, N.J.: Prentice-Hall, Inc.

Klein, D.M. 1983. Hands-on. *Engineering News Record,* May 12, 1983.

Kleinbaum, D.G., and Kupper, L.L. 1978. *Applied regression analysis and other multivariable methods.* North Scituate, Mass.: Duxbury Press.

Kraut, A. 1965. The study of role conflicts and their relationships to job satisfaction, tension, and performance. Unpublished Ph.D. dissertation, The University of Michigan.

Lagina, S.M. 1971. A computer program to diagnose anxiety levels. *Nursing Research* 20:484.

Lazarus, R.S. 1966. *Psychological stress and the coping process.* New York: McGraw-Hill.

Lazarus, R.S., and Averill, J.R. 1972. Emotion and cognition: with special reference to anxiety. In *Anxiety: Current Trends in Theory and Research,* vol. 2, ed. C.D. Spielberger. New York: Academic Press.

Lee, R.S. 1970. Social attitudes and the computer revolution. *Public Opinion Quarterly* 34:53–59.

Lefcourt, H.M. 1972. Recent developments in the study of locus of control. In *Progress in Experimental Psychological Research,* ed. B.A. Maher. New York: Academic Press.

Levitt, E.E. 1967. *The psychology of anxiety.* Indianapolis, Ind.: The Bobbs-Merrill Company, Inc.

Lichtman, D. 1979. Survey of educators' attitudes toward computers. *Creative Computing* 5:48–50.

Likert, R. 1961. *New patterns of management.* New York: McGraw-Hill.

Linn, R.L., and Slinde, J.A. 1977. The determination of the significance of change between pre and posttesting periods. *Review of Educational Research* 47:121–50.

Lord, F.M. 1963. Elementary models for measuring change. In *Problems in measuring change,* ed. C.W. Harris. Madison, Wis.: University of Wisconsin Press.

Lord, F., and Novick, M. 1968. *Statistical theories of mental test scores.* Reading, Mass.: Addison-Wesley.

Lucas, H.C. Jr. 1981. An experimental investigation of the use of computer-based graphics in decision making. *Management Science* 27:760.

Lusk, E.J., and Kersnick, M. 1979. The effects of cognitive style and report format on task performance: the MIS design consequence. *Management Science* 25:787–98.

Mason, R.I., and Mitroff, I. 1973. A program for research on management information systems. *Management Science* 19:475–87.

May, R. 1977. *The meaning of anxiety.* New York: W.W. Norton.

Meichenbaum, D.H. 1977. *Cognitive-behavior modification, an integrative approach.* New York: Plenum Press.

Naylor, F.D., and Guadry, E. 1973. The relationship of adjustment, anxiety, and intelligence to mathematics performance. *The Journal of Educational Research* 66:413–17.

Next magazine. 1981. "And Some Who May be Allergic...." May 1981, p. 94.

Nie, N.H.; Hull, C.H.; Jenkins, J.G.; Steinbrenner, K.; and Bent, D.H. 1975. *SPSS.* New York: McGraw-Hill.

Paul, L. 1982. Research on cyberphiliacs, cyberphobiacs reveals 30% of workers fear computers. *Computerworld* April 5, 1982.

Pedro, J.D.; Wolleat, P.; Fennema, E.; and Becker, A.D. 1981. Election of high school mathematics by females and males: attributions and attitudes. *American Educational Research Journal* 18:207–18.

Phares, E.J. 1976. *Locus of control in personality.* Morristown, N.J.: General Learning Press.

Raub, A.C. 1981. Correlates of computer anxiety in college students. Unpublished Ph.D. dissertation, University of Pennsylvania.

Resnick, H.; Viehe, J.; and Segal, S. 1982. Is math anxiety a local phenomenon? A study of prevalence and dimensionality. *Journal of Counseling Psychology* 29:39–47.

Robinson, J.P., and Shaver, R.P. 1973. *Measures of social psychological attitudes.* Ann Arbor, Mich.: Institute of Social Research.

Rosenman, R.H.; Friedman, M.; Strasu, R.; Jenkins, C.D.; Zyzanski, S.J.; and Wurm, M. 1970. Coronary heart disease in the Western Collaborative Group Study: a follow-up experience of 4-1/2 years. *Journal of Chronic Disease* 23:173–90.

Rotter, J.B. 1966. Generalized expectancies for internal versus external control of reinforcement. *Psychological Monographs: General and Applied* 80(1).

Rounds, J.B. Jr., and Hendel, D. 1980. Measurement and dimensionality of mathematics anxiety. *Journal of Counseling Psychology* 27:138–49.

Rout, L. 1982. Computer choler: many managers resist "paperless" technology for their own offices. *Wall Street Journal,* June 24, p. 1.

Sandberg-Diment, E. 1982. Personal computers: the children seem to know no fear. *The New York Times,* August 17, 1982.

Scheffe, H. 1959. *The analysis of variance.* New York: Wiley.

Shaffer, R.A. 1982*a*. Judgement day: the thinking computer arrives. *Wall Street Journal,* September 3, 1982, p. 14.

Shaffer, R.A. 1982*b*. As professional and business interest in personal computers swells.... *Wall Street Journal,* October 8, 1982, p. 35.

Shapiro, S.F. 1979. Quelling the fear of computers. *Journal of Technical Writing and Communication.*

Shouksmith, G. 1970. *Intelligence, creativity, and cognitive style.* New York: John Wiley and Sons.

Spielberger, C.D., ed. 1966. *Anxiety and behavior.* New York: Academic Press.

Spielberger, C.D.; Gorsuch, R.L.; and Lushene, R.E. 1970. *State-trait anxiety inventory manual.* Palo Alto, Calif.: Consulting Psychologists Press.

Sudweeks, R., and others. 1980. Development of the Syracuse mathematics anxiety scale. American Educational Research Association Meeting, Boston, MA. ERIC Document Reproduction Service No. ED 186 266.

Suinn, R.M. 1972. *Mathematics anxiety rating scale.* Ft. Collins, Colo.: Rocky Mountain Behavioral Institute.

Taylor, A.L. 1983. Finding the A on the keyboard. *Time* May 16, 1983.

Taylor, J.A. 1953. A personality scale of manifest anxiety. *Journal of Abnormal and Social Psychology* 48:285–90.

Teaching managers through computers. 1981. *Wall Street Journal,* December 11, 1981, p. 29.

Themes, Sr. E. 1982. Three methods of reducing math anxiety in women. Unpublished Ph.D. dissertation, Kent State University.

Titus, R.O. 1983. Overcoming computer phobia. *Interface Age* April 1983.

Tobias, S. 1978. *Overcoming math anxiety.* New York: W.W. Norton and Co.

Valecha, G.K., and Ostrom, T.M. 1974. An abbreviated measure of internal-external locus of control. *Journal of Personality Assessment* 38:369–76.

Weinberg, S.B. 1980. Identification of computer anxiety. Connecticut Research Foundation report 5170–000–22–0218–35–270.

———. 1983. Interviewed by Geoffry S. Howard, Saint Joseph's University, Philadelphia, Pa. April 8, 1983.

Weinberg, S.B., and English, J.T. 1983. Correlates of cyberphobia. Unpublished paper, Saint Joseph's University, Philadelphia, Pa.

Weinberg, S.B.; English, J.T.; and Mond, C.J. 1981. A strategem for reduction of cyberphobia. Proceedings of the AAAS Convention.

Winer, B.J. 1971. *Statistical Principles in experimental design.* New York: McGraw-Hill.

Witkin, H.A.; Oltman, P.K.; Raskin, E.; and Karp, S.A. 1971. *A manual for the embedded figures test.* Palo Alto, Calif.: Consulting Psychologists Press.

Wysocki, B. 1979. Automated offices: executives discover computers. *Wall Street Journal,* July 6, 1979, p. 1.

Zmud, R.W. 1980. The role of individual differences in MIS implementation success. *Proceedings of the 12th Annual Meeting of the American Institute for Decision Sciences* 1:215.

Zuckerman, M. 1960. The development of an affect adjective check list for the measurement of anxiety. *Journal of Counseling Psychology* 24:457–62.

Index